Douglas Hill

Fortune Telling

illustrated by John Beswick

Hamlyn Paperbacks

FOREWORD

Divination, prophecy, prediction, prognostication, fortune telling, all are words for man's perennial urge to find out what is to befall him. Sometimes there are subtle differences: prophecy usually implies an inspired person, speaking god-like of the future, while divination refers to some magical ritual performed to reveal what is to come. There is no need to quibble; it will be clear to which of these divisions each particular form belongs.

Divination must be humanity's oldest profession. No doubt as soon as early man developed a sense of time, he began to inquire about the future. No doubt also, a group of specialists sprang up instantly with the claim that they could answer those inquiries. So prediction and prophecy appears with professional status at the very threshold of recorded history, when other activities – which might vie for the title of 'oldest profession' – were still conducted on mainly an amateur level.

Certainly it is man's most specialized profession, having fragmented into countless intricate and arcane forms, rituals, techniques. Many of the most obscure of these have now died out, and only a sampling will be included here to hint at their curious variety. Other forms – some childishly simple, some vastly complicated, some millennia old and others relatively new – have never thrived so well as they do today. They will occupy the forefront of this survey of divination and fortune telling.

D. H.

Published by Hamlyn Paperbacks,
The Hamlyn Publishing Group Ltd,
Astronaut House, Feltham, Middlesex, England
In association with Sun Books Pty Ltd., Melbourne

Copyright © The Hamlyn Publishing Group Limited 1972
Reprinted 1982
ISBN 0 600 32835 X
Phototypeset by Filmtype Services Limited, Scarborough
Colour separations by Schwitter Limited, Zurich
Printed in Spain by Mateu Cromo, Madrid

CONTENTS

William the Conqueror stumbled upon landing – a bad omen

SIGNS AND PORTENTS

Ordinary folk beliefs, superstitions, are concerned with that elusive state of affairs we call luck. Everyone will have heard of the notion that 13 is unlucky, that a four-leaf clover confers luck. A surprising number of these beliefs concern *omens* – signs and warnings of good or bad luck to come.

Sometimes the omen – the action that foretells the future – is itself a bit of good or bad luck, here and now. Finding a coin is lucky in itself, but superstition says it is also an omen of future prosperity. Spilling salt or breaking a mirror are also obviously unlucky accidents, and at the same time are serious omens of ill luck to come. Stumbling or tripping at the beginning of any enterprise is a bit of unlucky clumsiness that is also a symbolic foreshadowing of ill fortune.

The meanings and associations of other omens may not always be so obvious – and quite often can be in dispute. America and most other countries share the belief that a black

cat crossing one's path is unlucky. The British see good luck in it, and bad luck in white cats. Some folklore traditions say an itchy ear signifies misfortune approaching; others insist it means the approach of good news. Generally, a strange dog following one home brings good luck, but for gamblers, fishermen and others encountering a dog is the worst luck. If the insect called a ladybird lands on someone, it is often said to be lucky, especially if it has seven spots; but some say it is unlucky unless it flies off when the old rhyme ('Ladybird, ladybird, fly away home') is spoken.

And so on. A catalogue of such omens and their differing meanings could be endless. Many people could extend it with their own personal omens that are found in no traditions. Among my own friends is a man who feels his day will be unlucky if his phone rings before 10 am, and a lady writer who sees a dire omen if the 'x' on her typewriter sticks. However, we must stay in the realm of traditional, shared superstitions, many of which focus specifically on the most crucial moments of human life – birth, marriage and death.

5

Ghanaian pre-birth charm

Omens at Birth

A baby is born, and superstitious folk begin at once to look for signs of its future. A caesarian confers good luck on a baby, and so does an extra toe or finger. The baby will be lucky if the mother's head pointed 'north' during labour; and pioneer Americans said it was lucky to be born in a covered wagon. Being born with teeth means a baby will grow up to be a murderer (or a vampire, in Eastern Europe).

The time of birth is also important, though not so crucial as in astrology. Most will know the ancient rhyme: 'Monday's child is fair of face, Tuesday's child is full of grace; Wednesday's child is full of woe, Thursday's child has far to go; Friday's child is loving and giving, Saturday's works hard for a living; the child born on the Sabbath Day is blithe and bonny, good and gay'.

Folklore adds that babies born on New Year's Day will be lucky; born on Christmas, will have occult powers; born in May, will be sickly. American superstition says those born on March 21 will have terrible luck, and those born between June 23 and July 23 will fail in life. Generally a child born under the new moon is believed to become physically strong in future, but a child born between the disappearance of the old moon and the emergence of the new will not live past puberty. A newborn will be unlucky if the moon shines on it. European folklore says that babies born under a waxing moon will be boys; only girls are born under the waning moon. Babies born at ebb tide will not live long – though some traditions say that they *cannot* be born at the ebb, that ebb tide is the time of death, flood tide for birth. A sunrise birth supposedly means good luck, a sunset birth means laziness, an early morning birth is an omen of longevity.

Many omens carry on through stages of infancy. For instance at the christening it is a good omen if the baby cries, a bad omen if the clergyman makes an error in the ceremony. Eastern American belief states that a child must fall out of bed three times at least, and fall downstairs once, before it is one year old, or it will be an ignoramus. It is an ill omen if the child develops unusually, talking before walking or the like.

Hei-tiki – Maori charm for the spirit of an unborn child

Irishwomen watching apple peel for a marriage prediction

Marital Prediction

Traditional folklore always sees woman solely in the role of wife and homebody. So, if a girl had nothing to look forward to but marriage, she began looking forward to it however she could, as with simple forms of marriage divination.

Some of these rituals are supposed to induce a dream vision of the husband-to-be. An American method requires the girl to gaze at a bright star, wink three times, then go to bed. In Britain the night of January 20 is St Agnes' Eve when – as in Keats's poem – girls may dream of their future husbands. Modern girls may still sleep with bits of someone else's wedding cake under their pillows, to bring on such dreams.

Other rituals reveal the names or initials of future bridegrooms. Strong-minded girls might try catching a snail on All Hallows and keeping it in a flat dish overnight; its slime trail is supposed to trace out the giveaway initial. A portentous initial will also be formed if a girl can peel an apple without breaking the peel, then let it drop over her left shoulder.

Sometimes a girl may perform certain rituals after which the first eligible man she meets will be the one she will marry. She may wear a four-leaf clover in her shoe, or hang over her door a pea pod with nine peas, or count seven stars on seven successive nights. Frantically complicated counting rituals seem to be favourites. Practices reported from America include counting 100 red convertibles, or counting car licences containing numbers in threes – 000, 111, etc., up to 999.

There are omens simply indicating whether a girl will marry, and when. The number of nails in a horseshoe, or eggs in a bird's nest, indicate how many years she must wait. If the first person she sees outside her house on Valentine's Day is a man, she will be married within three months. The Halloween game is still played where boys and girls each tie an apple to a string and whirl it around. Whoever owned the first apple to fall off will marry first. The last to fall belongs to one who will never marry.

Children ducking for apples: Halloween marriage divining

Omens of Death

Marriage divination is one thing, but no one is likely to perform rituals that foretell his death. All the same, folklore provides enough *spontaneous* omens to satisfy any morbid curiosity. Many involve animals, because of the old notion that animals can sense the approach of the Grim Reaper; so the best known death omen in most lands is the howling of a dog outside a house at night. A live adder on the doorstep also foretells a death in the house, and so does a crow flying three times over the house, a raven croaking or an owl hooting near the house, a white pigeon on the chimney. There are omens from the plant world too: a flower blooming out of season, a white bean plant in the garden, one apple remaining on an apple tree, are all death portents. As for ordinary domestic articles, death is foretold if a picture falls, untouched, from its nail, if scissors fall point down when dropped accidentally, if a candle burns blue. Less homely, but ranking with the howling dog for universality, is the omen seen in the tolling of a church bell when no one has rung it.

Most of the foregoing are signs applying to a house or a family. Other omens can be taken personally by an individual, and some are themselves linked with death. One is doomed to die soon if one stumbles at a funeral, or is the last person to be spoken to by a dying man. Otherwise, a superstitious man may see a sign of his own death in the sight of a falling star, if he hears a ringing in his ears, if a black beetle runs over his shoe, if he hears a cock crow at midnight.

Several noble families have traditions that the head of the family receives a special death warning, like the banshee that screams in ancestral Irish homes, or the phantom Drummer of Airlie that appears to the dying laird in a Perthshire family. A lord or commoner alike may be warned by seeing an apparition of himself – the fearsome *doppelganger,* ominously called the 'fetch' in Ireland. Apparently Queen Elizabeth I saw such a vision, as did Catherine the Great. But then when the death of monarchs is foretold, it is (or was) an omen of national disaster, something more than ordinary death omens.

Scottish phantom drummer, a 'fetch' who in legend is said to appear at the death of the head of the Airlie family

Portents of Cataclysm

The death of kings, and general upheaval in nations, is most often foretold in superstition by omens of some enormity, like an eclipse. The sun was eclipsed before the death of Queen Catherine of England in the 16th century, while three 'suns' appeared in the sky prior to the execution of Charles I in 1649. A monarch will supposedly die, also, if all the bay trees in the land wither, or if special bodies of water inexplicably dry up – like the pool in Devon that is said to have dried up before George VI died in 1952.

Similarly awe-inspiring omens are associated with natural calamities. A golden ring round the moon supposedly warns of hurricanes, in some regions; in America, a comet has been a sign variously of pestilence, flood, even the end of the world. Meteorites ('falling stars') are said to portend plague or famine or the like. At other times these disasters can be predicted, superstition says, by more trivial omens. British lore says the blooming of violets out of season signifies the coming of pestilence. Unusual restlessness among cattle is an omen of earthquakes; the departure of crows from a favourite wood indicates coming famine. The Aurora Borealis, a commonplace

A Bayeux tapestry depiction of an ominous comet in 1066

Turks firing at the moon to halt an eclipse (19th century)

sight on winter nights in northern lands, is taken as an omen of war when appearing unusually far south.

War is the man-made catastrophe that matches all the natural ones, and numerous omens predict its coming. A vast increase in the number of rats in a community, or the number of lambs born, or the number of boy babies born, all are taken as omens of war. Cosmic magnificences serve the same purpose: some say an eclipse in 1914 provided an omen of World War I, but others saw such an omen a few years earlier with the appearance of Halley's Comet. The appearance of a red moon also supposedly means war is imminent, as does the vision of a strange heart-shape in the northwestern sky.

Superstition invariably tends to overbalance towards gloom and pessimism, preferring to provide hosts of omens of bad luck. So it is not surprising that there are few clear omens to look for that signify *peace*, in wartime. One such is, if rare, at least also romantic: peace is heralded by the appearance of a complete rainbow in the sky, during war or moments of international crisis.

SPECIALIZED SEERS

The ordinary omens of good or ill fortune were always the property of every and any man, and of course they remain so. But from the most ancient times, seeing the future came to involve more than merely reading the small, accidental omens that anyone might gather. It came to demand the operation of definite techniques and skills, developed by certain specialists.

These were the shamans, the medicine men, the witch doctors, the priests, who were seeking to impose order and system on the scattered arrays of chance omens – so that interpretation would come to be standardized, invariable, and therefore able to be passed on within the closed realm of the shaman or priest. (They were often passed on as secret teachings, to ensure that the shaman would retain his status and his employment.) So more and more complex methods began to emerge, curious rituals demanding special equipment, some training, and considerable supernatural know-how.

Of course there were still the individualist seers, not shamans but strange gifted beings (sometimes associated with the priesthood as oracles, but at other times just self-employed soothsayers) whose utterances were believed to be inspired by gods or demons to foreshadow the future. Aside from these, the ordinary man still had his homely superstitions. So no one had to go without a reading of the future.

But with the rise of things like Chaldean astrology or Egyptian dream interpretation or Chinese techniques of divination from tortoise shells, the specialists came to be very much in charge. Monarchs and rich and important people would hardly bother with ordinary omens when all that expertise was available. So the specialized rituals received patronage and became thoroughly established. And so they remain – no longer wholly secret, in this age of publicity, but still the property of the professional diviners.

The priestess of the Delphic Oracle was under the aegis of the god Apollo, but was often called 'Pythia' or 'Pythoness' to link her with an older snake-god of Delphi

The Augurs of Rome

A fine example of how omens became specialized into a complex divinatory art comes from ancient Rome, where a special group of diviners was set up by the government to take omens that would predict the outcome of any civic action. They were called *augurs*; and though augury can mean many kinds of divination, the Roman augurs were especially devoted to 'ornithomancy', reading the future from birds.

As we have seen, birds also figure largely in the common omens of popular superstition: hearing the first cuckoo of spring on the right is good luck, eagles flying low over a plain are an omen of war. The Roman augurs took their omens from, in many cases, equally straightforward occurrences, but dressed them up with preparatory ritual. The omen-taking usually happened on a special hilltop, where the augur marked out a special section of the sky to be watched (by waving his magical staff, the *lituus*) for bird activity within it.

Vultures and ravens, woodpeckers and ospreys, eagles (the bird of Jupiter) and owls (of Minerva) were prominent among the most significant omen carriers. Birds flying east were a good omen; birds flying low and seemingly directionless were a bad omen; birds being extremely active in purposeful ways hinted at excessive human action to come, such as war. A crow cawing on the left was favourable, and so was a raven's croak from the right. And so it went – with the most unbelievable complications and variations and additions as the years went by and the 'College of Augurs' grew more and more specialized.

Today ornithomancy remains functional only in a few isolated superstitions. We, for instance, have the jaunty superstition that being struck by pigeon droppings is good luck – because of an unlikely legend that a man so struck in Monte Carlo went on to break the bank. But the augurs saw omens in every kind of dropping, and in the position, shape, size, colour, texture and more. They also read the future from shed feathers, frequency and loudness of bird calls, rapidity of wingbeat and so on. Finally it all became overloaded: one set of omens would be qualified by another until the future could not be read – and, in the end, the system fell into disuse.

Roman augur examining the flight of ravens for signs of the future, often from the most minute details

Babylonian clay model of a liver used to teach hepatoscopy

Haruspicy

The word 'augury' was also often applied to another leading form of ancient divination, from the entrails of animals (properly called 'haruspicy'). The animals chosen were usually sacrifices to the gods, and so were believed to have the gods' cryptic messages written on the inner organs. But some peoples preferred to read the entrails of fish, frogs and other unlikely creatures. Ancient Babylon developed the technique in general, and it was highly popular among the Greeks, Romans and Etruscans. Primitives have used it as well, in Africa and Borneo and elsewhere, while the Aztecs sometimes read the future from *human* entrails.

Little precise detail has come down to us about the meanings of various signs read from the entrails. But it is known, for instance, that an extremely dire omen was indicated if an important organ should appear to be entirely missing. One legend asserts that two oxen sacrificed just before the assassination of Julius Caesar were found to lack hearts. Equally unfortunate omens were taken from any excessive bloodiness about the entrails, or any unusually livid coloration. And it portended disaster if the diviner let the entrails fall to the ground while examining them.

'Hepatoscopy', divination by liver markings, was a branch of haruspicy that came nearly to dominate the method. Clay models of sheeps' livers, dating from Babylonian times and probably used as teaching aids, contain the most complex divisions and markings of the surface of the organ. One Etruscan model of a liver is divided into 40 zones, each connected with a specific god; the interpreters looked for special vein formations and odd textures, within each zone, perhaps to find shapes resembling symbols that were particular to each god. Along with the liver, the gall bladder was vitally important: if swollen, for example, it foretold good fortune. But then entrail divination was rarely that simple – and, like augury by birds, it acquired the most cumbersome burden of over-complication and unnecessary technical detail, which undoubtedly aided the decline that it had undergone by the early fifth century A.D.

Roman bas-relief of diviners examining a bull's entrails

The Voice of the Gods

If a man in ancient Greece could afford it, he might do without common practices like entrail or bird divination and go to one of the famous shrines where a priestess with special powers would provide him (for a fee) with oracles – which were direct messages from whichever god was the patron of that particular shrine. It might have been Zeus, in many cases – there was even a combined Greek-Egyptian oracle where Zeus was identified with the Egyptian deity Amon. The shrine at Dodona in Greece was dedicated to Zeus; there the priestess stood beneath a 'prophetic oak' and delivered her oracles, which some said were communicated by the rustlings of leaves. The greatest oracle of all was dedicated to Apollo, and was situated on the flank of Mount Parnassus, at Delphi.

Apparently Delphi was a holy place even in Mycenean days, nearly 1000 years before the great days of ancient Greece. And the oracle was delivering its pronouncements still, centuries after those great days. The peak of its fame and wealth came during the sixth century B.C., when monarchs and generals and the rich and important of all lands consulted it, and when it had a longstanding reputation for infallibility that gave it great power in the Greek state and society.

Certainly the aura of infallibility must have been aided by the potent ceremonies that accompanied the oracular statements. The Pythia, as the Delphic priestess was called, went through purifying rituals to prepare her, and some hallucinogenic agents were probably involved. Then a bull or goat was sacrificed, incense and other perfumes burnt, and – with the client hidden, watching, awaiting answers to his questions – the priestess would enter a trance state. She would tremble, foam at the mouth, tear her clothing, and finally mutter a few words or sounds. Acolytes would note these, which would constitute the day's prophecy, supposedly direct from Apollo speaking through the Pythia's mouth. Often it would be so cryptic as to appear meaningless – but meaning would be imposed later (a technique not unknown to today's fortune tellers) to link the oracle with events as they happened. At other times the oracle could be decidedly ambiguous, as in the famous case of King Croesus, who asked about the outcome of a war he wanted to wage against a neighbouring nation. The oracle informed him that if he went to war he would destroy an empire. Encouraged, Croesus began his invasion. And shortly an empire had, indeed, been destroyed – but it was the empire of Croesus.

Painted bowl from fifth century B.C. Greece showing the visit of the Athenian king, Aegeus, to the Delphic Oracle

Ask the Dead

The word 'necromancy' is often taken to mean the general conjuring up of spirits and raising of the dead, and is even used as a synonym for all black magic. It properly means divination by the dead – though of course they must first be re-animated. Primitives believed that the dead acquired special magical powers including seeing the future; the old civilizations shared this belief, and so the death-obsessed Egyptians, for instance, knew many dark rituals that would supposedly enable the preserved bodies called mummies to speak the future. Greece and Rome knew of the practice, too: the Roman writer Lucan described the success of a witch in calling back life into a dead body so that it could answer the questions of Pompey.

This is, of course, the form that divination by the dead usually takes: the reanimated corpse (or conjured-up spirit) must answer the questions put to it by the magician. Then sorcerers have been supposed to have other, more nefarious purposes for raising the dead. The creatures so resurrected become the black magician's slave, as with the legendary *zombis* of Haitian voodoo lore. No one ever thought of asking these monsters questions about the future, it seems; they were mainly believed to be nothing more than cheap labour.

Traditionally, the dead were also believed to be specially able to reveal the whereabouts of buried treasure, which may have made it all worthwhile for necromancers. Certainly the magical textbooks indicate that reanimating a corpse was one of the ugliest and most protracted of all black-magic rites. It involved much distasteful preparation – abstaining from salt, eating dog's flesh and the like — along with wearing grave clothes removed from a corpse. Some recipes insist that the body to be reanimated must be embraced by the magician, or mutilated or otherwise interfered with in various gruesome ways.

Apparently it is slightly less unpleasant, and less difficult, to conjure up a ghost or a spirit. Such manifestations overcome the need to plunder a grave, and they do the prophetic job adequately.

The ghost of Samuel, conjured up for Saul by the Witch of Endor, predicting Saul's downfall

Modern Necromancy

The recalling of the spirits of the dead must be one of the oldest forms of magic; certainly our primitive forebears spent much time seeking favours of the deceased ancestors. Then there was Saul going to the Witch of Endor to call up the spirit of Samuel; and Odysseus, in Homer's *Odyssey,* conjuring up the ghost of the seer Tiresias, to prophesy. In more recent times, it was said that Dr Dee, court astrologer to Elizabeth I, called up a spirit with the help of his unpleasant assistant Kelley; while the notable 19th-century French occultist Eliphas Lévi also claimed to have raised a spirit – but said that he fainted with exhaustion and fright before he could ask it any questions.

Today not even the most advanced cults claim to be able to raise the dead. But the modern cult of Spiritualism has at least this in common with necromancy: it will often answer questions, including those about the future, supposedly by messages from the dead. Human 'mediums' transmit the messages; so do the ouija board, planchette and so on, mechanical manifestations of the spirits. The ouija board has the

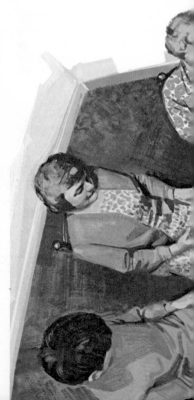

alphabet round its perimeter; a counter points to various letters though under no (apparent) control by participants. The planchette is a wheeled contrivance bearing a pencil, on which the medium's hand rests lightly while it scrawls 'spirit messages'. Both are used today for the more shallow kind of fortune telling – often, regrettably, by children. The *séance*, with the medium in trance supposedly acting as mouthpiece for the dead, can also be a fortune-telling technique, but is mainly used as such by the hordes of frauds and charlatans who infest the practice. Serious mediums eschew prophecy, and seek (they say) to establish communication with the dead, to comfort the bereaved and to prove survival after death. But many also claim to be *clairvoyants* (see page 61).

Left, Dr Dee and Edward Kelley, Elizabethan magicians and necromancers; below, the circle of a modern spiritualist séance

LOOK TO THE STARS

Prehistoric man may have concluded that the lights in the sky had something to do with his life – for after all everything else did. Much later, the ancient Mesopotamian civilizations organized this attitude into a system of belief, based on the notion that everything in the universe has some connection with everything else. This idea was the foundation of astrology when it was still one with the youthful science of astronomy. It was a belief shared by the magicians and philosophers who developed astrology throughout the world – in ancient Egypt and Persia, China and India, Greece and Rome. In classical times astronomy came into its own along with the other sciences, and occult astrology split away. It continued to thrive, and has flourished in all centuries since.

Nor has it changed a great deal over the millennia, except to grow ever more complex and intricate. The 16th, 17th and 18th centuries were responsible for much of this – a time when

Ancient Zodiac figures; far right, a Mesopotamian priest

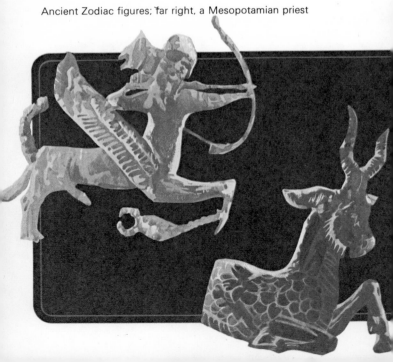

every royal court had its own astrologer (like Dr Dee for Elizabeth I) and when horoscopes were gospel to most people, enough to make Londoners riot in panic for days when astrologer William Whiston predicted the end of the world in 1736. The 19th century brought the publication of some of the modern world's most extensive texts of astrology, and made the practice into the common man's favourite. Today every popular newspaper and magazine carries instant horoscopes; great statesmen, financiers and other leaders of men are revealed as avid followers of their stars; and the current craze for the occult among the international 'underground' of young people has pushed astrology to even dizzier heights. The number of practising astrologers in Europe and America is unquestionably in the hundreds of thousands, while no one could estimate those practising in Asia – especially India. Clearly astrology is the modern world's most popular and most lucrative form of divination.

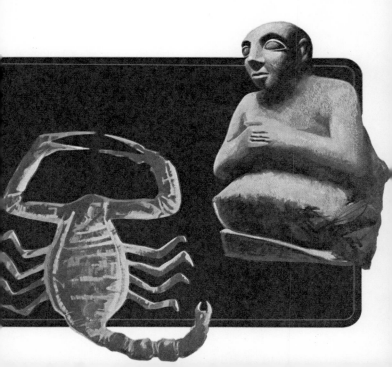

Aries

Taurus

Gemini

Cancer

Leo

Signs of the Zodiac

The zodiac is an imaginary strip of sky representing the sun's path round the earth. (Astrology still works on the basis of the earth at the *centre* of things.) Within this strip, which is also the apparent path of the planets, lie twelve constellations – the signs. At different times of year the sun is said to be 'in' one or another of the signs; so your birth date, even without a horoscope, shows your birth sign. Associated with the signs are various characteristics, aspects of personality, which are supposed to be discernible in people according to the month of their birth – though one's astrological character is composed of many more factors in the horoscope. The following is a capsule account of astrology's general view of the 12 zodiacal types.

Aries the Ram (Mar 21–Apr 20). Restless, creative.

Virgo

Taurus the Bull (Apr 21–May 21). Steady, reliable.

Gemini the Twins (May 22–June 21). Intellectual, contradictory.

Cancer the Crab (June 22–Jul 22). Sensitive, introverted.

Leo the Lion (Jul 23–Aug 23). Ambitious, powerful.

Virgo the Virgin (Aug 24–Sept 23). Neat, logical.

Libra the Scales (Sept 24–Oct 23). Humanist, well balanced.

Scorpio the Scorpion (Oct 24–Nov 22). Sexy, sinister.

Sagittarius the Archer (Nov 23–Dec 21). Gregarious.

Capricorn the Goat (Dec 22–Jan 20). Independent, pessimistic.

Aquarius the Water Carrier (Jan 21–Feb 19). Spiritual, revolutionary.

Pisces the Fishes (Feb 20–Mar 20). Vague, tolerant, artistic.

Representations of the modern Zodiac signs from Aries (top left) to Pisces (top right) with their symbols used in horoscopes

Pisces

Aquarius

Capricorn

Sagittarius

Scorpio

Libra

A 17th-century illustration of the 'earth-centred' universe

The Ascendant

Astrology columns in the popular periodicals base their vague and over-generalized bits of prediction on nothing more than the birth sign, or sun-sign. Which should mean that everyone born within the same month should have alarmingly similar personalities and life patterns. Those casters of horoscopes who take themselves rather more seriously reject this simplified newspaper astrology. Reading character or the future in the stars, they say, demands a complex juggling and weighing of a great many interrelated factors – of which the sun-sign is but one, and not even the most important one.

If any one factor deserves to be singled out as the most crucial, it would be the one called the 'ascendant' – meaning the sign of the zodiac that was rising above the horizon at the moment of birth. Of course the horoscope depends on a knowledge of the exact moment of birth, so that the month-wide spread of the sun-sign seems imprecise indeed. Astrological texts compare the importance of the ascendant, the rising sign, to that of the sun-sign by showing the two as they are in certain giveaway horoscopes – like that of Edgar Allan Poe, whose birth sign was the generally positive Aquarius but whose ascendant was Scorpio, with all the morbid and gloomy qualities that fit the author's mastery of the horror story.

Aside from sun-sign and ascendant, the sign at 'midheaven' (at the 12 o'clock position, if the horoscope is seen as a clock face) is of some importance in the overall picture. But then the relative importance of the signs can be dictated by more than their own positions. The position of the *planets* 'in' the signs affects their meanings and contributions, all the more because each sign has its own 'ruling' planet.

Below, passers-by in a British street market examine the ready-made, 'instant' horoscopes on sale

YOUR
HOROSCOPE
IS
COMPILED
BY MADA

The Planets in Astrology

The planets too have their special characteristics, which supposedly leave their marks on the human temperament in terms of their position in the horoscope. It should be noted that the sun and moon have been included as planets since ancient times, and so the practice must be perpetuated even today when we know that the one is a star and the other a satellite. If astrology has not kept up with the times in this regard, it has at least tried to come to terms with the three planets discovered in fairly recent years, Uranus, Neptune and Pluto. Still these newcomers do not seem entirely at home in horoscopes, nor are astrologers entirely in agreement about their meanings.

The following capsule summaries of the ten planets and their qualities include mention of the zodiac signs that are variously 'ruled' by them.

Sun (Leo). Most important of the planets, its influence reaches back to ancient sun-worshipping days. Powerful, energetic, dominating.

Moon (Cancer). Probably the third most important factor in a horoscope, after ascendant and sun position. Changeable, emotional, often irrational.

Mercury (Gemini and Virgo). Concerned with communication. Clever, often unreliable – 'mercurial'.

Venus (Taurus and Libra). Planet of love and eroticism.

Mars (Aries and Scorpio). Violent, aggressive.

Jupiter (Pisces and Sagittarius). Expansive, extraverted, domineering.

Saturn (Capricorn and Aquarius). Cautious, gloomy, associated with ill fortune and so very important in horoscopes.

Uranus (discovered 1781, said to have taken over Aquarius). Associated with technology, social reform, revolution.

Neptune (discovered 1846, said to have taken over Pisces). Associated with mysticism and occultism.

Pluto (discovered 1930, said to have taken over Scorpio). Gloomy, dark, associated with repression and death.

In astrology the moon is connected with irrationality (note our word 'lunacy') and femininity. This 17th-century print shows a group of 'moon-struck' women

The Rest of the Horoscope

The astrologer drawing up a horoscope, having assembled all the signs and planets in their places, still lacks all the information that he must have before interpreting it. He must next measure the angles between the planets, called 'aspects', which reveal the planets' interrelationships. Remember that the earth is the centre of the horoscopic circle; the whole is of course 360°. The angles are measured to within about 10° of error – for if they had to be exact, there would be rather fewer aspects.

Conjunction means two planets near one another – within the 10°. Two similar planets, both favourable or unfavourable, would enhance each other in this aspect. *Opposition* shows two planets at opposite sides of the circle. Jupiter in opposition to Saturn would tend to cancel one another out. *Sextile* occurs with two planets 60° apart, and is usually said to be a favourable aspect, whatever planets are involved. So is *trine,* a 120° angle between planets. *Square* means planets 90° apart, and is generally considered unfavourable, as is *semi-square,* 45°. Other minor aspects, concerning angles of less rounded numbers, are mostly just extra fussiness and complication, beloved by astrologers but not demanding our attention here.

The astrologer is also concerned with the twelve *houses,* which are arbitrary divisions of the horoscopic circle into fixed portions. Different systems of division exist, with the

The four elements of antiquity – air, water, fire, earth

simplest (twelve equal portions) generally the least favoured. But no matter where astrologers place the 'cusps' (boundaries between houses) they usually agree on the associations given to the houses, as follows:

First house: personal being, life pattern.
Second: possessions and finances.
Third: Education and social relationships.
Fourth: Family background.
Fifth: Love, sex, pleasures.
Sixth: Health, domestic life.
Seventh: Marriage, partnerships, enemies.
Eighth: Death, inheritances.
Ninth: Spiritual and religious life, travels.
Tenth: Profession or occupation, community life.
Eleventh: Friends, aims and goals.
Twelfth: Difficulties and obstacles.

Wherever the signs and planets fall in regard to these areas, they can be linked to particular segments of one's life.

With this element in the horoscope, the assemblage is complete, ready for interpretation. Other relationships exist, such as the groupings of the signs in terms of the four elements of the ancient world – but such refinements are not of paramount importance in giving the broad picture, at least, of an individual's character and potential as the stars – and the interpreting astrologer – reveal them.

Reading the Stars

Putting together a horoscope may be a somewhat laborious task, but by no means insuperably difficult. You begin with the moment of birth, as precise as possible. Then after making some adjustments to allow for geographical variation you use printed compilations – called 'ephemerides' and 'tables of houses' – that tell you where the planets were, and what sign was in the ascendant, at that moment. It all requires a bit of arithmetic and a bit of concentration, but any astrological text can teach most people to cast a horoscope in a very short time. The *skill,* if skill there is, enters when the astrologer turns to interpreting the horoscope.

As it happens, a great many people get by as professional astrologers simply by having read a number of the best known texts, thus assimilating a basic knowledge of what all the relationships within a horoscope supposedly mean. Then the interpretive process simply requires some practice in juggling and fitting together. One's sun in Aries might indicate a certain restlessness that is rendered more creative by the moon in Cancer or a Piscean ascendant: and so on. The reading can go many ways, and within the framework of the traditional meanings there is plenty of room for the astrologer to operate, to justify giving weight to this item and deprecating that in order to achieve a suitable overall picture.

This method, by which one can arrive at pretty well whatever reading will please the client, has been called 'cookbook astrology', and is the kind most widely practised by 'professionals' who cast individual horoscopes for a fee. They usually do so from no knowledge of a client save the birth date; and in most cases the interpretations will be generalized and vague enough to leave room for the client to read his own case into the material. When the interpretation suggests (for example) that the client has potential for success and the good life, if he doesn't let lack of confidence get in the way, most people would be likely to nod and say, 'That's me, all right'. (Or anyway this might be said by most people of the sort who commission horoscopes on this level.) There are a few astrological people whose approach tends to resemble modern psychiatry or psychoanalysis more than fortune telling. They insist on background information, even interviews with clients – because for them the horoscope merely focuses and confirms their *intuition* about individuals, a skill at assessing people that few own, that can be developed (they say) but not taught to someone who lacks the potential. The skilled psychoanalyst may use the interpretation of dreams to focus a similar practised intuition. Remember that the astrologer on this level is mainly reading character. *Prediction* by horoscope is usually the province of the 'cookbook' professional.

Prince Charles's visibly royal horoscope — Leo in ascendant

Progressing Horoscopes

On the popular level, then, astrology is fortune telling. Professionals who do cookbook readings may claim to be analyzing character, but one's 'fortunes' – future potential and likely development – are implicit, as are hints and guidelines for the future, however oblique. The glib, meaningless generalities that pass for astrology in newspaper columns also claim to be seeing the future, showing you what the stars foretell for you next month, next week or tomorrow.

Some astrologers claim that a study of planetary positions at the time of President Kennedy's birth would have indicated that on the day he died Dallas was the only place in the United States where assassination was possible

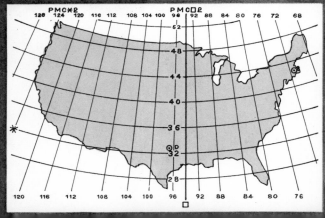

A more explicit form of prediction occurs in astrology – not based on a horoscope for the moment of birth, which contains only *im*plicitly the person's future, as a seed contains the plant. The professional astrologer will advance time by drawing up a horoscope *for* the future. The technique is called 'progressing' the horoscope, and there are various methods for performing it. A common way draws up a horoscope for specific days after birth corresponding to specific years in the future: so a horoscope for the twenty-first day after birth would be interpreted as revealing the twenty-first year of the infant's life. Or the astrologer could find (in the ephemerides) the positions of the planets at certain points in the future, to locate the so-called 'transits' – when the planets will pass over various delicate points on the horoscope and have definite future effects. Thus a person might be told that his sun-sign is Scorpio, and that in his forty-ninth year Saturn will pass through a conjunction with the sun, creating many dire and unpleasant developments in his life.

This kind of prediction is fairly safe: any accident or setback during the given year will seem to verify it. More particularized prediction – in this year you will be married, in that year war will break out – cannot rely so easily on coincidence. Yet astrological records show a legion of such predictions that came off – including a 16th-century foreglimpse of the French Revolution by an astrologer named Turrel, or Kepler's prediction in 1563 of the Great Plague of 1665, or a British almanac's warning of a royal death in the year that Edward VII died. But then rather more instances of failed predictions might be flaunted – like all those British astrological assertions in 1939 that there would be no war. Perhaps it boils down to the fact that, in enough tries at prediction, any astrologer will make some hits. But is it only coincidence? Statistics gathered over years by the French writer Michel Gauquelin hint at surprising veracity in astrology's reading of character potential. Gauquelin found that in thousands of cases men in certain professions shared certain horoscopic features – Mars appeared prominently for soldiers, Jupiter for politicians and so on, just as the cookbooks have said for centuries. Such studies are hardly conclusive, though, as buttresses to the whole vast, magical superstructure.

The Uses of Astrology

In our time and for centuries before us, the main function of astrology has been the provision of horoscopes for ordinary individuals. Astrology has also continued, on a smaller scale, to fulfil its more ancient function (as in Babylon) of drawing up horoscopes for nations and their rulers. Not that there are many rulers today who want horoscopes; but the astrologers draw them up anyway, in the astrological journals, for every new president or prime minister, and also for every new nation whose 'birth date' equals the first moment of independence.

Horoscopes can serve other special purposes too. There is the once popular form called 'horary' astrology, which purports to answer your specific questions by casting horoscopes for the moment of asking. Serious astrologers decry this as mere parlour magic, and they also dislike the 'electional' form of astrology, which determines auspicious moments (by the stars and planets) for important events like marriages and coronations. This form is in special favour still in India, where

A Hindu holy man, who will consult the stars before any important decision or action

top politicians make their moves by the stars. Astrology also finds its way, as further variation, into other forms of fortune telling – cards, palmistry, and more – where the signs of the zodiac are associated with special configurations that appear in these allied arts.

A fortune teller outside an Italian law court, approached by people wanting to know in advance the outcome of court cases, by means of 'horary' astrology

Medical Astrology

Another use for the 'science' of astrology had its heyday in past centuries, when doctors considered a knowledge of the stars to be a necessary part of their education. Throughout European history the twelve signs have been associated with twelve separate areas of the body and afflictions thereof. Aries rules the head, Taurus the throat, Gemini the lungs and so on down to Pisces and the feet. These relationships are traditionally represented by illustrations of the Zodiac Man, Homo Signorum, who appears in all the ancient astrological texts and a surprising number of modern ones.

The planets too reveal their medical associations, partly through their rulership of certain signs but also on their own. The changeable moon is associated with changes in the health generally, but also with diseases of the 'left-hand side' and of the womb. Mercury has a tie-up with speech impediments and mania; Mars is naturally linked with fevers, though it has been said that if Mars is not in your ascendant you are safe from smallpox without vaccination.

Astrological auspices were important to past physicians, especially when letting blood was universally thought to be a valid curative; astrology showed the best times for the bleeding. So it did for other kinds of operations: a 16th-century text warns against operating on a part of the body on a day when the moon is in that part's ruling sign. Even in the early years of this century astrological medicine cropped up in the writings of an American astrologer who believed, among other things, that surgical operations are best conducted when the moon is waning.

So, indeed, astrology still clings to medicine's coattails. Books on astrological diagnosis (the most common form today of medical astrology) still flow from the occultist presses, and doctors can be found who firmly believe (for instance) in twelve 'cell salts' related to the zodiac signs and to cures of the parts of the body linked with the signs. Of course the occult has always played its part in diagnosing human ills, and medical applications will be found (as later pages will indicate) within most of the divinatory arts.

The stars and the body, shown on the 'Zodiac Man'

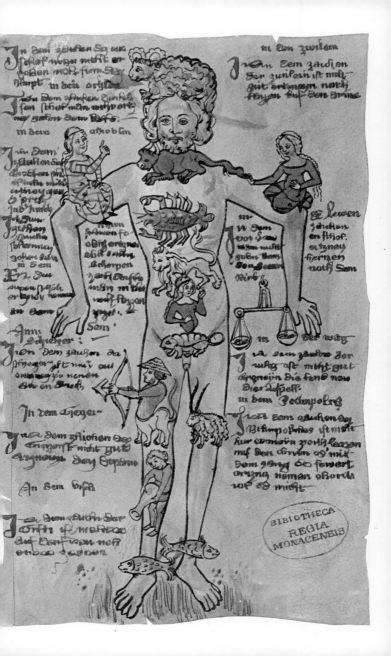

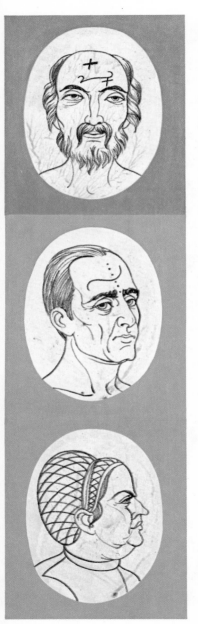

FORTUNES IN FACES

Astrological character reading is just another way of categorizing people into types – pigeon-holing them by personality. Through the centuries astrologers have suggested that one's astrological type shows in one's face and form, for which the usual word is *physiognomy*. So a person with a strong moon in his horoscope is moon-faced, a Taurus type is thickset and bullish, and so on. Some ancient physiognomists were carried away, on occasion, and fancifully suggested that Capricorns should have goatish faces, Cancers should walk with a 'crabbed' gait, and similar correlations. But fortunes can be told (and futures implied) from faces without reference to the stars. We still look for character in faces, seeing a weakling in every receding chin, an intellectual in every high forehead, a deceiver in every pair of close-set eyes – although

Examples of physiognomical prediction from the 17th century. Top to bottom, the forehead of a poisoner; the forehead of an unstable person; and the face and nose of an arrogant woman such ideas have no basis in fact. In the past, physiognomical fortune telling went further. Old texts of physiognomy are full of unsettling drawings, showing in gross caricature the thick lips of a lustful man, the protruding teeth of the choleric, the pointed nose of an arrogant woman, bristly hair on an arrogant man, the turned-up nose of a vain man, and more. Some of the illustrations can be a trifle unexpected. The chin of an impotent man is shown to be firm and cleft; the nose of a magnanimous man is beaked and immense (so much for the anti-semites' fallacy); the eyelashes of a malicious man are thick and long; and the eyes of an ignorant man are seen as deepset and brooding. Weak characters, in a 16th-century text, have long hair; ruthlessness shows in a thick beard, malice in heavy eyebrows. Clear eyes, big noses and rounded foreheads denote nice people, it seems, every time.

More 17th-century divination by physiognomy. Top to bottom, the forehead of a man doomed to suffer a head wound; the forehead of an adventurer; and the rather up-to-date hair of a weak character

Marks and Blemishes

Still on the subject of the face and form, a person's character and fortunes were often read in the 16th and 17th centuries from some of the more usual skin markings, primarily moles but also lines or creases. Once again astrology can be dragged in to help: various facial moles have their horoscopic connections, such as a mole on the upper lip with Aquarius, on the nose with Libra, on the right cheekbone with Scorpio, on the neck with Saturn. Neck moles were dire signs even without astrology, being said at one time to foretell imprisonment, at another to be an omen of decapitation. Moles on the belly

Facial moles and their traditional links with astrology

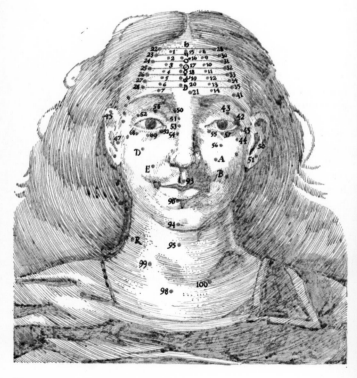

reveal voraciousness, on the lips gluttony, on the ear good luck. As for the future, moles on the loins predict bad luck, on the chest mean poverty, on the upper leg mean riches, on the hands indicate many children.

Metoscopy, which is the art of reading futures in lines on the forehead, can also bring in astrology, for the seven main horizontal lines equal the seven main planets, Saturn at the top down to the moon above the nose. Also a man's temperament can be seen physiognomically in forehead markings. Three high horizontal lines indicate peace and gentleness, but beware unstable finances and possible head wounds; three lines on the central or lower area indicate aggression, even murderousness; a vertical line cutting through three cross lines means longevity, and a diagonal line shows a man is an adventurer. Two well spaced horizontal lines on a woman's forehead foretell her happiness and good fortune. One line only, across a man's forehead, means he will be successful in war. As one more example, curious *wavy* lines on a forehead indicate that the head's owner will die by drowning.

A 17th-century depiction of the principal moles on the body

47

The phrenologist — an 18th-century satiric cartoon

Bumps on the Head

Phrenology began with Dr Franz Joseph Gall, born in Baden in the 18th century, a student of the older physiognomists with whom he shared the precept that physical features reflect psychological ones. Gall became especially interested in relationships between skull shapes reflecting *brain* shapes which in turn reflect the nature of the *mind*. From these roots he developed the 'science' of phrenology.

Basically, it asserts that various faculties of the mind (Gall said 37, but they were later extended to 42 and more) can be seen as separable, and as contained in differentiated parts of the brain, called 'organs'. The organs affect the size and shape of the exterior of the cranium, in their own localities. Therefore the development of these faculties in an individual mind can be 'read' by means of cranial measurements. The faculties include some fairly obvious ones – Combativeness, Benevolence, Spirituality – but also some more obscure ones, like Adhesiveness (which is in fact Friendship) and Amativeness (different from Adhesiveness *and* from Conjugality). The organs reflecting social and domestic faculties are at the back of the head, those of personal aspiration at the crown, those of religion and morality at the top. The phrenologist also attends to skull size, the distance between the eyes, and so on, as indications of character. The practitioner himself must have a well developed faculty of Size – which with Weight and Form and the like can be found above the eyes.

Phrenology gained a tremendous following in Europe, Britain and America in the early 19th century. Out of the fad, predictably, grew the popularizers, the backstreet or peripatetic 'head-readers'. This degrading, plus wrangling within the movement and massed attacks from religion and medicine, contributed to its decline after the 1850s. Phrenology groups can still be found in larger western capitals, but generally – like its precursor physiognomy but *un*like its cousin palmistry – it is now almost entirely faded.

The 'organs' of the brain and their various 'faculties'

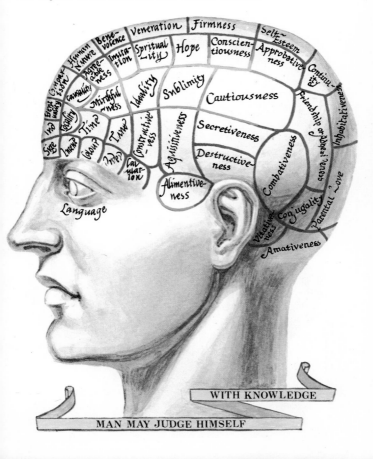

DIVINATION BY HAND

Most people call it palmistry, but it is wrong to think that only the palm of the hand is read in this form of divination. Its more self-conscious names include 'chirognomy' (reading character in the hand) and 'chiromancy' (reading futures in the hand). Practitioners feel that the art must have begun in the mists of prehistory, but the earliest western mention of it occurs in Aristotle (fourth century B.C.), although it has undoubtedly had a longer history in China and India.

The Romans carried it on from Greece, and it found itself eventually in medieval Europe, where a handful of 13th and 14th-century manuscripts, mostly written by monks, form

The Hindu god Siva, with clear palm lines on one hand

A Roman hand in bronze, with symbolic decorations

the basis of the tradition. Many Renaissance intellectuals took up chiromancy along with astrology, alchemy and so on, and the status of names like Michael Scot or Paracelsus helped to establish it in later centuries as a primary form of divination. So it remains today, probably next in importance, or at least in popularity, after astrology – certainly as widespread, among amateur do-it-yourself diviners, as cartomancy or other forms requiring little or no equipment and only a superficial knowledge of 'cookbook' interpretations. Palmistry of course gains extra charisma by its long association with the romantic gypsies, who are often mistakenly thought to have cornered the market on this practice. Leading professionals, among them the famous Cheiro (Count Louis Hamon) who dominated 19th-century British palmistry, have tended to sneer at back-street fortune telling behind the bead curtain, along with amateur parlour-magic palm reading. In fact this is precisely the type of palmistry that has lasted best into our time. While a few psychologists and the like have shown an interest in chirognomy (as will be seen shortly), it has certainly not attracted the widespread academic and philosophical attention that has been given to astrology. Perhaps its mystique, its association with arcane occult mystery, is not so fully developed. Unpretentious people might find this praiseworthy.

The fingers and the principal 'mounts' of the hand, in palmistry, with their astrological connections.

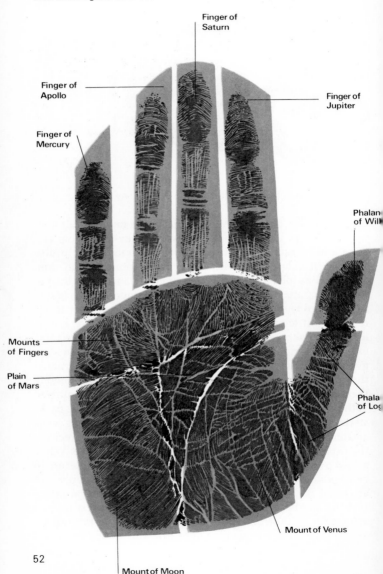

Finger of Saturn

Finger of Apollo

Finger of Jupiter

Finger of Mercury

Phalan
of Wil

Mounts
of Fingers

Plain
of Mars

Phala
of Log

Mount of Venus

Mount of Moon

Parts of the Hand

In chirognomy, before looking at lines on the palm certain readings can be made from the general shape of the hand and its parts, indicating the character and future tendencies of the person. There are seven basic shapes of hands: the primitive or elemental, thick and crude; the spatulate, spade-shaped, showing energy and cleverness; the square, showing practicality; the 'philosophical', rather knobbly, showing rationality and sometimes pedantry; the long artistic hand, also showing intellectualism; the shapely 'idealistic', showing dreaminess and perhaps a psychic ability; and, seventh, the mixed hands with more than one of these qualities.

The fingers, and pads of flesh beneath them called 'mounts', bring astrology into palmistry: the usual textbook meanings of the planets inform the meanings of these parts. But the shapes of fingers can be read otherwise. Large fingers reveal a certain slowness and patience, short fingers mean impatience, fingers both thick and short can indicate selfishness. Crooked fingers hint at a tendency to malice, thick puffy fingers reveal a concern for fleshly pleasures, smooth fingers mean an intuitive ability, widely separated fingers show a love of independence. A large thumb means general capability and forcefulness, and is supposedly to be found on notably successful people. For that matter, there are complex meanings ascribed to each joint or phalange of the thumb, which space limitations do not allow to be included here. According to Fred Gettings in *The Book of the Hand* (Hamlyn, 1965), Chinese palmistry traditions include a vastly intricate system of chirognomy based on the capillaries of the thumb's first joint.

A firm palm indicates a strong, energetic person, while a flabby palm shows passivity. Thin, dry palms reveal nervousness; thick, soft palms indicate sensuality; hollow palms with poorly defined mounts show a tendency towards illness.

Markings on the fingernails are often read by palmists as other indications of illness; but then fingernail marks form a special kind of fortune telling of their own, called onychomancy (see page 136). Serious palmists ignore such frills. After examining the shape of the hand, its parts including the planetary links of the mounts, they get on with the important job of reading the lines of the palm.

Lines of the Hand

The Life line takes precedence, since its length is said to show length of life and health – though palmists prefer not to tell clients when they will die, even if they ask. For those with morbid curiosities, the usual method is to divide a print of your palm into ten equal parts, each representing ten years of life. If your Life line ends in the seventh segment, you will reach your three score and ten.

Many other points can be taken from the Life line, as from the others: for instance, a reddish colour in the Life line means strength tending towards aggression. But only the main points can be touched on here. The Head line should be clear and well defined to reveal a clear and high intelligence; if it curves towards the mount of the moon imagination will be highly developed, even too highly. The Heart line traditionally refers to one's love life; for the most satisfying kind the line should rise from the mount of Jupiter. Sometimes the Head and Heart lines are not distinct, but run together (mind and

Palmistry's usual view of the lines and zones of the hand

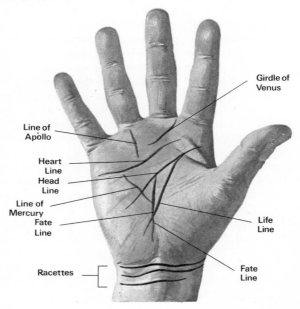

Girdle of
Venus

Line of
Apollo

Heart
Line

Head
Line

Line of
Mercury

Fate
Line

Racettes

Life
Line

Fate
Line

THE LINES OF THE HAND

emotion not separated). The result is called the 'simian' line, and supposedly shows some kind of abnormality or even degeneracy – idiocy, criminality, fanaticism, and the like.

More briefly now, other important lines include the Fate line, reaching towards the finger of Saturn, which is vital to prophetic palmistry (it indicates those future developments regarding success and riches); the 'girdle of Venus', across the finger mounts, reveals your emotionality; the line of Apollo, if clear, shows the presence of creativity; the line of Mercury indicates clairvoyant abilities. The wrist lines often called 'rascettes' can reveal the prospects of fulfilled ambition (if the right wrist's marks are strongest) and of a good marriage (if the lines run from wrist to mount of Jupiter). Also, specific marks on any line – breaks, spots, forks, crosses and so on – have their meanings. A break is generally ill omened, a fork means a confict of interest, a cross means a forthcoming shock (in the area of life governed by the specific line), a wave means a likelihood of change. A doubling of any line reinforces whatever meaning can be gained from the reading of that line.

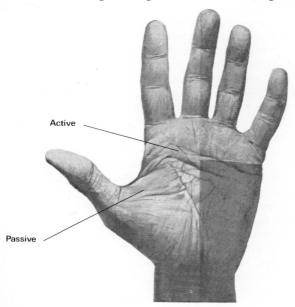

Active

Passive

OUTER   INNER

Palmistry and Science

If germs of truth were to be found in any forms of fortune telling, common sense would say that palmistry might be among them – for it would seem more likely that something of ourselves should be inscribed on our skin, rather than being discernible in the movements of constellations millions of light-years away, or in the shapes of bovine guts. At least the practice of fingerprinting shows (as chiromancers delightedly say) that our hands do have some measure of individuality. But it is a long way from police fingerprint files to prediction

Still, grist has been brought to modern chiromancy's mill by researchers like Julius Spier of Germany, who gathered sheaves of children's handprints and sought to relate psychological assessments to chiromantic ones. Similar statistical forays in Britain and America have brought out some interesting points, mainly concerning the 'simian' line mentioned before. This feature occurs again and again among special groups of people, pronouncedly among mongoloids; and Australian findings showed it to be prominent in children suffering from leukemia. In 1966 some New York doctors found correlations between the simian line (and other markings, like a high Y-shape in the junction of the three main palm lines) and babies whose mothers had had German measles during pregnancy, a major cause of abnormal births. So the palm print could be an invaluable early warning of hidden abnormality. Also, American doctors at Tulane University found that patients born with certain heart defects also had certain complex distortions in the palm lines, not found among people who contracted heart disease in later life. Chromosome disorders are also reflected in palms.

Not only the hands enter into this parade of scientific interest. The ancient Chinese read the feet as well as the hands – and according to Sybil Leek, modern expert on witchcraft and divination, a Los Angeles pediatrician who for some reason has collected footprints of children in his care has found that he can systematize the prints and *predict* accurately the illnesses a child would contract. Whether or not these findings – which are of course far from conclusive – amount to a vindication of chiromancy must depend on how convinced or sceptical one was to begin with.

Palmistry today has lost none of its popularity

Analyzing Handwriting

From reading hands, it is a short step to reading the marks made by hands. Graphology is rarely presented as a form of prognostication; it is a technique for reading *character* (just as astrology, palmistry and the rest claim to be, for much of the time) and the prediction is implied, indirect, growing out of the idea that the character analysis indicates future behaviour. Not that graphology can be an acceptable substitute for psychological investigation: like other ways of interpreting character on a fortune telling level, it has been weighed down with assorted arbitrary rules for interpretation, no less convincing than those of any popular divination – even though some may have come down from graphology's beginnings (as the invention of a 17th-century Italian philosopher named Aldorisio).

The popular manuals direct the budding graphologist to notice margins, spacing and straightness of lines, pressure and of course legibility (if any) aside from the formation of the words and letters. As for the last, the usual rules say that a

For analysis of handwriting, look for different slants, tight or loose spacing, legibility and more

slant to the right means an outgoing, active person, and to the left means caution and discipline; but if either slant is too extreme, they show insecurity and arrogance respectively. An excess of flourishes means insincerity, too much simplicity reveals sloppiness. Extra full loops on 'l', 'h', etc., show heartiness – but sensuousness if on lower loops like 'g' or 'y'. The signature reveals a forceful personality if underlined, a reserved one if smaller than normal script, a pedantic one if abnormally legible.

Pop graphologists do warn that people can consciously alter or recreate their script, and so can 'lie' about themselves graphologically. Even with such reservations, it all seems rather a banal, ineffective kind of amateur analysis. One do-it-yourself manual adds to this impression by offering some questions that graphology might answer about you: 'Am I broadminded?' 'What sort of person should I marry?' and, pathetically 'Am I normal?' But the mere fact of one's turning to graphology should answer that one.

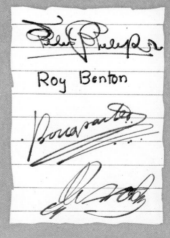

Note, top, the strong upper and lower loops. Right, some typical variations in signatures

WHO HAS THE SIGHT

Foretelling the future without recourse to specialized equipment and involved systems of interpretation is supposed to consist simply of *seeing* ahead in time, which is called precognition. It in turn is a form of clairvoyance, meaning clear seeing, which is a major part of what our time has come to know as extra-sensory perception (ESP). It has other, more traditional names – second sight, psychic power – and has been one of the mainstays of shamans and magicians through the ages. The primitive shamans saw it as a special dispensation from the gods, a divine visual message to be seen only by the specially favoured. We think of it, if at all, as a unique and rather freaky talent, erratic and uncontrollable. It leads to the kind of specific prophecy in which Cassandra and Tiresias specialized, in Greek legend – and also like that made by Apollonius of Tyana, when he predicted the murder of the Roman emperor Domitian and also 'saw' the killing itself, from many miles away. It also can lead to the kind of specific prophecy contained in a 'vision' – not just the Old Testament type, but of the sort that comes unbidden to ordinary people, according to hosts of books on ESP.

Clairvoyance today is a vital aspect of modern fortune telling and occultism generally; spiritualist mediums claim the gift, in many instances, and it is not always clear whether the message to the medium's client comes from clairvoyance or from the dear departed. Other fortune tellers may use horoscopes, crystal balls, Tarot cards or whatever, for their reading of the future, but many proponents of ESP (and many believers in divination, too) have suggested that these methods and bits of equipment are merely reinforcements or 'focusing' aids (fine tuners, as it were) of a talent for clairvoyance. Indeed, this suggestion contains the implication that ungarnished clairvoyance has always been the *only* way of seeing the future, and that all the ritual comes unnecessarily from man's love of magical mystification.

A shaman of a primitive Finno-Ugric tribe from northern Europe. Like most other primitive priests or witch doctors he believes his prophetic power comes from the gods

Clairvoyants in Action

A man writing in the American magazine *Fate* once proffered some steps by which anyone could learn to be clairvoyant. The process involved some odd and jumbled exercises which need not occupy us here. But the learning may be unnecessary, by virtue of the number of people who have experienced apparently spontaneous clairvoyant visions, which come to be collected in psychical research or folklore. As one example, there was an R.A.F. wing commander during the last war who found himself with the horrifying ability to see the 'mark of death' on his fellow pilots, before flights from which those

The famous medium Eusapia Palladino, 'levitating' a table

'Random selection' machine used in modern ESP research

pilots never returned. Clairvoyance has often functioned, for non-professionals, to provide warnings or practical hints. It can also operate, say parapsychologists who follow in the footsteps of the great J. B. Rhine, for more prosaic purposes – like the extra-sensory reading of special cards in another room.

The seeing of professional clairvoyants tends to be more restricted: their clients seek extra-sensory or divinatory messages, and messages they get. Often enough they are the usual fortune telling patter: business will be good, October will be a threatening time, beware of a tall dark stranger. Techniques differ: some clairvoyants require an interview or some prior knowledge of the client, at the least, but the others can rattle off instant readings. These are the more impressive, since clever questioning in an interview can elicit much useful data for the 'seeing'. But the British clairvoyant Maurice Woodruff, among other top-level diviners, does not even let a client speak to him before he begins the reading.

Other clairvoyants claim to perform by means of 'astral projection' (their astral selves flit about to do the seeing) while many, including clairvoyant spiritualists, need merely enter a trance state, or at the least undergo some form of light auto-hypnosis. Leading seers like Woodruff manage to 'see' from full consciousness.

Psychometry

The point has been made that much fortune telling which uses special equipment like the crystal ball may be actually clairvoyance, and that the crystal or whatever serves only to stimulate and channel the seer's ESP. The implication then is that all this traditional paraphernalia, carrying with it the imprint of magic and occultism, might be dispensed with if the user could bring his clairvoyance into action without external aids. Even then perhaps one sort of aid to the seeing, used by a great many clairvoyants, could not so easily be put aside. This is usually an object related somehow to the subject that is to be seen. Touching it induces the clairvoyant vision – so it is known as an 'inductor', and its use is generally called psychometry.

Perhaps no non-professional clairvoyant has gained more fame in our time than a Dutchman named Gerard Croiset – a non-professional because he does not do readings for fees, but works within the auspices of Utrecht University's ultra-respectable Parapsychology Institute. Croiset, now in his sixties, has performed in many experiments and tests set up by the Institute – but has also given his time to help people outside the university. Though a mere request for help over the telephone has called up clairvoyant visions for him, he prefers when possible to use an inductor. He is especially famous for finding lost children, and uses some possession of the child's to call up a vision of the period of time when the child was lost. Touching a possession of a dead person has shown Croiset the cause and time of death, and he has often aided the police of many European countries, and also of America and even Singapore. One feat of his may have opened a whole new area – psychometric paleontology? – when he touched a fossilized fragment of bone and was able to 'see' a long extinct animal in its prehistoric setting. His talent can overcome time in the other direction too: in many tests he has been shown one chair in an empty hall before a public meeting, and has accurately described the person – in appearance and also details of personal life – who would sit in that chair during the meeting.

The hectic clairvoyant life of Gerard Croiset

The Divining Rod

Though water divining, or dowsing as it is more usually called, is clearly a form of ESP, it may not readily appear to belong in a discussion of fortune telling. However, divining, or divination, means perceiving that which is hidden – whether in time or space. Also, the traditions of dowsing do not restrict it merely to finding water courses or wells. Like necromancy, it is famed in legend for turning up the hiding places of buried treasure, and people still use it today to locate lost objects. In every case, when the dowser points to a spot and says 'Look there' or 'Dig here' he is making a *prediction*.

The dowser of folklore uses a forked hazel twig, holding the two branches in his hands and waiting for the treasure or whatever to drag down the other end, mysteriously, irresistibly. Modern dowsers use sophisticated metal rods, which perform the same way. Behind the various forms of rods, like antennae, is the specially attuned 'receiver' of the gifted dowser, who is clearly a clairvoyant. The most talented dowsers claim an ability to change channels on their inner receivers – to look for water one day, coal the next, metal the next, and perhaps Granny's lost teeth the next. Some dowsers approach the realm of medical prognostication by dowsing over an ill person to locate the whereabouts of the illness and to identify it. Then again a respectable British archaeologist has used the divining rods to discover suitable diggings – and has usually succeeded in predicting the location of Roman sites. Another British dowser named W. H. Burgoyne has often been involved in searches for the bodies of drowned persons – and has sometimes been brought in to do so by officialdom, just as a 17th-century French dowser named Jacques Aymar used his talent to track down the occasional criminal when requested to do so by the police. In modern America many city corporations and private industries use dowsers to locate underground pipes, cables, water supplies, etc. In short, there is no end to what the dowser can look for and claim to find; and his claims seem to be coming true often enough to interest non-committed scientists.

The dowser's traditional implement – a forked hazel twig

Radiesthesia

In our technological age, some dowsers have replaced yesterday's forked twig with a more streamlined and efficient pendulum – small weights on thread, which swing or come to rest to reveal the presence of whatever is being located. At the same time, these dowsers often like to work at their ease – by passing their pendulums or other equally handy devices over maps, while comfortably seated at home. No walking over damp, chilly fields looking for underground water. Sometimes they will check their map readings, by visiting the sites in person with their locating instrument, but more often they let the client do the outside work.

Many dowsers are convinced that their extra-sensory ability has to do with picking up otherwise imperceptible 'radiations' given off by the substance being searched for. They then prefer to call their trade 'radiesthesia'. And while ordinary dowsers might use any kind of implement – a plain pencil, balanced across a finger, for instance – the radiesthesist shows a marked preference for pendulums, used in concert with a rule or graded disc so that the pendulum can point to precise gradations. At times the term radiesthesia is reserved especially for those efforts with the pendulum which concern *medical* matters – the location and diagnosis of disease. The pendulum is passed over a sufferer's body, and his ailment, it seems, makes itself known to the handler. Radiesthesists can also diagnose, it is claimed, without the patient's presence – by passing the pendulum over a urine or blood sample. Or it can be passed over a photograph of the patient, presumably a similar process to dowsing for water from a map.

In recent years some radiesthesists have abandoned balanced implements in favour of machines that pick up diagnostic vibrations, from the patient or from some sympathetic-magic part of him like a blood spot. The psychiatrist D. J. West has described one such machine as consisting of 'an impressive array of knobs and dials and little else'. Then perhaps this form of technological ESP is not all that far, after all, from conventional occultism like a crystal ball.

A radiesthesist holds a needle over a patient's wrist

THE MAGIC CRYSTAL

Crystallomancy, better known as crystal gazing, has had a long and impressive history. As far as Europe is concerned, it made its first major appearance among the Merovingians (or Franks) in the early Christian era: archaeologists of past centuries found quantities of small crystal balls in the widespread burial grounds of the Franks. The older traditions of many primitives include divination by the crystal: Borneo, New Guinea and Madagascar tribesmen, Australian aborigines, the Mayas and the Incas, and several American Indian tribes including the Cherokee.

In Europe, at first, crystal gazing was a minor branch of a broader kind of divination that involved peering into reflecting substances, like water, mirrors and so on (for which see later). The magic crystal soon overtook these other forms; in the 16th century, Queen Elizabeth's court magician Dr Dee had a crystal which he called his 'shewstone' and on which he placed considerable value. By the 17th century it was *de rigueur* for any occultist, whether a professional sorcerer or a scholarly dabbler, to have a crystal somewhere about the place – which he would have called a 'speculum'.

By the 19th century the crystal had acquired its position of prominence within the field of fortune telling that it holds today – as widespread as astrology, palmistry or cards. Some of the reason for its popularity is, of course, the extreme simplicity it involves. Buying a glass ball (upwards from £2 in Britain for one four inches in diameter) and sitting staring into it is hardly taxing; all you need then is the gift of clairvoyance (or, as the sceptics would say, a good line of patter). Aside from plain clairvoyance itself, there is probably no simpler form of fortune telling today.

Yet occultists have invariably gone to great pains – as they usually like to do – to impose quantities of special requirements and rituals upon this most straightforward of divinatory techniques.

The paraphernalia of crystal gazing – the round table standing in a magic circle, its top engraved with mystic names, the candles, the crystal on its special mount

Rituals of the Crystal

You can use a glass sphere, but perfectionists prefer true crystal – quartz, or (even better) beryl, which has some mystic associations. You can just hold it in your hand, but purists insist on special mounts to hold it on a table with a white cloth. Some also demand a frame enclosing the ball, of ivory if possible, engraved with magic names like Adonay or Tetragrammaton. For these people the table should be circular, with more mystic engravings on it, and should hold gilt candlesticks with lit candles. Elsewhere in the room incense might burn. You should have prepared the crystal by washing it purifyingly with alcohol or vinegar; you should have also purified yourself by washing, various abstentions, special incantations and perhaps a herbal infusion. All the foregoing should be done while the moon is waxing; the actual gazing works best at sunrise, midday or sunset, and under the zodiac sign of Libra.

Then you sit down and look at the crystal ball. You may or may not enter a trance state; experts differ on this, some thinking in terms of slight auto-hypnosis. You will have to wait a few minutes, then you will begin to see things. Centuries ago it was thought that you would see a spirit (or demon) first, who would show you the scenes you wanted. Today's crystal gazers generally think in terms of ESP (clairvoyance) and not spirits; they see visions without supernatural intermediaries. They may see mere cloudiness: white clouds bode well, black are evil, green or blue are good omens, red or yellow portend disaster. They may see specific scenes, pictures from elsewhere in time or space. These may be on the level of 'I see a tall dark stranger' or may be strikingly detailed visions that are open to being checked (as, apparently, are many of those mentioned in T. Besterman's book on crystal gazing). Otherwise you may see certain symbolic shapes that have come, as such symbols do, to take on fixed, rote meanings. So a globe within the globe foretells travel; a star means success, or a warning; an eye may mean good luck but (depending on atmosphere) can also mean impending evil; a bird means a message; and a skull, obviously, bodes no good at all.

Simplified use of the crystal – and the omen of a skull

FATE IN THE DREGS

It will have become clear by now that much fortune telling requires interpretation – by standardized rules, secret knowledge or 'intuition' – of omens to be found in *random* occurrences. They may be bird flight or entrails, the casting of lots (to be looked at shortly) or the arrangement of tea leaves within an emptied cup. Some authorities insist that these leaves (and all the other random happenings used by diviners) serve only to channel a clairvoyant vision, acting merely as a starting point like the vague shapes discernible in a crystal ball. Nevertheless, there are countless possibilities in the shapes and forms that the leaves may take and the meanings which tea-room occultists derive from them.

So fill your teacup without a strainer, and either drink the tea or swirl it around (to spread the leaves) and pour it off. Immediately some general indications can be noted. Leaves close to the top concern events near in time, while those close to the handle concern matters close to home. The bottom of the cup is the area of ill omen. Generally dots mean financial gain, circles mean completion, straight lines mean direct progress. More specific shapes, of recognizable objects, can be looked for, of which the following is a selection.

Seeing an *airplane* shape can mean promotion, but if other leaves crowd round it (like clouds) it means danger and obstacles. An *anchor* shape means success or, at the top, love. A *bell* is a good omen, often of marriage. *Birds* on the right, or flying towards the handle, are a positive omen; but specific

Tea-cup reading, and some of the shapes that may appear

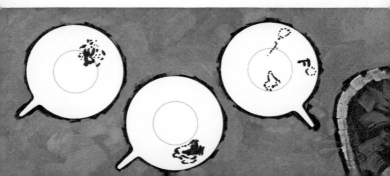

birds (like specific animals or flowers) have their own omens, if the species can be distinguished. An *eagle* means fame and success, a *raven* means trouble, a *peacock* means vanity and a *parrot* means slander. A *boot* at the top means travel. A *clock* means sickness, death if at the bottom. A *dog* can mean faithfulness, or a friend in need; of other animals, a *horse* galloping points to good news, or to a lover if just a horse's head, and a *lion* at the top shows strong positive influences on your side. An *egg* is an omen of success and joy. A human *face* means a setback, low in the cup, but elsewhere means a mere change. *Flowers* are good signs except at the bottom, where they mean illness; of specific varieties, a *daisy* means happiness, a *rose* means success, a *bouquet* means fulfilment. A *key* can mean improved business, but robbery at the bottom. A *ladder*, predictably, means advancement. A *mountain*, if clearly seen, means a journey. A *nun* may mean sorrow. A *parasol* suggests a lover. A *ring*, of course, speaks of a betrothal. A *scythe* means danger. A *snake* signifies enmity. A *star* means great good fortune. *Wings* are messages, good news if at the top.

Tea-leaf readers suggest adjusting these meanings to the individuality of the client; but clearly the human faculty of projection, of seeing what one wants to see, will provide all the adjustment necessary for anxious minds.

Variations on Tea Leaves

If you use teabags, or never drink tea, you still need not be deprived of omens from materials available in your own kitchen. Some fortune tellers burn herbs and read the ashes, calling it 'botanomancy'; others decapitate an egg and drip the yolk onto white paper to read the splatter. (For that matter, diviners have for centuries dripped hot wax or molten lead into cold water and read omens from the shapes – very akin to tea-leaf shapes – made by the sudden congealing.) Today one of the most prominent alternatives involves the use of coffee grounds. You may simply use the bottom of your breakfast cup, if you do not use some form of strainer. Or you can use the older, ritual method that requires much special cleansing, drying, then boiling in water of the grounds, after which the mixture is poured onto a white plate and swirled slowly around so that the water runs off and the grounds gradually sink, to stick on the surface in a useful scattering.

For interpretation, you may apply the usual means of tea-leaf shapes, but there are a few especially oriented to coffee. Wavy lines mean a journey, a slanting line warns of business failure, a square means joy, a triangle means unexpected luck, a circle with a dot or dots in it foretells a baby (a boy if three dots), a cross may mean the death of a loved one. But two crosses mean long life, and three indicate high achievement. (Some handbooks always see suffering or death in a cross, however many.)

With coffee, as with tea or any of the aforementioned drippings, it is usually said that a symbol may be altered by the presence near it of other symbols. A ring is a sign of engagement or marriage, but a cross near it warns of a broken engagement. A house means a change of address, and a triangle near it means the new property will be inherited. Dashes around the house warn of trouble in the present home. A ship means travel; but a cross near it means a journey because of a death in the family. More generally, watch out for the letter M: someone is trying to kill you.

Other typical tea-leaf shapes. Top, a bouquet and a heart can be seen; centre, a tree, a triangle, a windmill and a ship. Below, shapes can be detected in coffee grounds

WHAT DREAMS MAY COME

From the very earliest times men were convinced that their dreams could and usually did foreshadow future events. For that matter, people continue to hold this view of dreams in modern times, though with certain qualifications – for instance, none of the modern believers would assert that *every* dream is predictive. But some are, they would insist, though they would use the term 'precognitive', lent to them by modern parapsychology.

As terminology, this may not be any more informative or satisfying than calling a dream a vision sent by the gods or

A depiction of Jacob's Old Testament dream of the ladder

Thothmes' dream — the falcon-headed Egyptian sun-god Ra

spirits (good or bad), which is the definition generally used by the ancients. Indeed, the ancient peoples thought that dreams were often actual visitations of the spirits or gods; and that the dream which revealed the future might often feature a major deity playing a central role, speaking directly to the dreamer. In the ancient Mesopotamian *Epic of Gilgamesh* the hero's friend dreams prophetically of his own death, imaged by his being carried off by the god of the underworld. An Egyptian citizen named Thothmes dreamed of the sun-god Ra telling him he would be Pharaoh, which came true. In the Old Testament, Jacob dreamed of his famous ladder and of the destiny God had planned for him; in the New Testament, Joseph married the already pregnant Mary because God in a dream told him to.

Among more recent cases of precognitive dreams – often well attested, because the dreamer confided his dream to reliable witnesses before it came true – one might cite Abraham Lincoln's dream warning of his own assassination, or the famous dream of the Austrian bishop that foresaw the killing of Archduke Franz Ferdinand (which sparked off the first world war). Then there are the many accounts of precognitive dreams about the sinking of the *Titanic* in 1912 – including *two* such dreams on successive nights by an Englishman, Hon. J. Cannon Middleton. So it seems that, while gods and spirits may no longer be delivering them, the messages are still coming through.

The ancient Greek god of healing and medicine, Asclepios

Interpreting Dreams

The ancient world well knew that the meanings contained in dreams were not always immediately apparent; the gods did not always appear in person, or make themselves clear. Sometimes the meanings, the predictions, were buried in cryptic, symbolic visions. Then they needed interpreting, by means of the art called 'oneiromancy'. Remember Joseph's interpretation (in Genesis) of Pharaoh's dream of the fat and the lean kine. That story, of course, was told from the Hebrew point of view; otherwise, the Egyptians never seemed to need anyone's help in deciphering dreams, for some of the oldest recorded dream interpretations occur in Egyptian papyri. There, for instance, to dream of sawing wood foreshadows the death of your enemies, but to dream of teeth falling out predicts your own murder by your dependants. The dream of a snake signified good fortune, or the end of a dispute.

The old civilizations also made use of prophetic dreams in the practice of *incubation,* used to diagnose diseases and find cures. The Greek god of healing Asclepios functioned in this way; his priests would provide the ritual preparations and so on for a sufferer to have a special dream in the god's temple. The priests also interpreted the dream, plucking from it the diagnosis and prescription of the cure. Incubation was also practised in ancient China, Assyria and Egypt – while in Greece, sailors often slept in a temple of the sea-god Poseidon, before a voyage, hoping to dream prophetically of the nature of the voyage and any likelihood of danger.

The meanings of dreams soon became standardized and fixed in lists contained in handbooks. In the second century A.D. a Roman named Artemidorus put all later fortune tellers into his debt by gathering up meanings from more ancient Egyptian and Greek traditions and incorporating them into one massive 'dream book' that was being reprinted in Europe 1500 years later – and that is still being pilfered from by modern oneiromants. The next pages provide a tasting sample of such interpretations, past and present.

Omens and Symbols

All dream books since Artemidorus are merely compilations of standard omens, akin to many of those at which we looked in

Dream scene in an 'incubation' temple of Asclepios

the opening pages of this book: a dream of this means a wedding, a dream of that means a death. The compilations, from one year or century to another, do not always agree: if you are keen enough, or worried enough, you can always find a meaning that suits you, in some book somewhere. The amount of correlated agreement that does occur, over the centuries, shows how much each compiler seemed to depend on his predecessors. The following samples are taken mainly from omens and symbols on which there is fairly widespread agreement.

Some are obvious to the point of banality, as when a dream of gold means impending riches, or a dream of a storm means trouble coming. Many compilers play up the element of *reversal* (perhaps to soothe anxious dreamers); so to dream of being dead portends long life, to dream of being cursed (or crucified) means fulfilled ambitions, to dream of wearing ragged clothing means an end to your troubles.

Rather more often, the associations of omen and meaning can appear to be nonsensical, or surrealist. So a dream of your head being scratched means deception. A dream of flying: loss of possessions. Of eating books: imminent death. Of

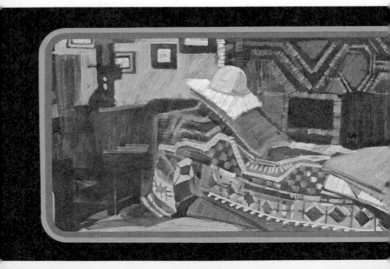

marriage: a change of address. Of milk: thwarting of plots against you. Of burning incense: danger. Of holding nails: attacks by enemies. Of purple cloth: illness. Of holding or cooking eggs: quarrels and sadness. Of washing your hands: end of a troubled time.

In the 20th century the interpretation of dreams has reached far more respectable levels. Sigmund Freud's development of psychoanalysis showed that dreams could often reveal the repressions, buried urges, unfulfilled wishes and so on that lie at the root of neurosis. C. G. Jung, who took depth psychology even further, found in our dreams the great symbols, universal to all mankind, which he called 'archetypes', and which also reveal the state of a mind's development when interpreted in individual terms. So perhaps dreams can foretell the future – if only by portraying some of the psychological paths a dreamer may be taking.

Sigmund Freud — and the couch on which his patients revealed their inner lives, and especially their dreams

THE MYSTERY OF NUMBERS

Numerology assures us that character can be delineated, the future read and other magics performed by the manipulation of simple numbers. In modern degenerate forms numerology is a collection of standard meanings, much like dream books, but it was once a matter of high mysticism. It reached its highest in the hands of Pythagoras, sixth-century B.C. Greek founder of a school that believed (to simplify somewhat) it was possible to express all things, and relationships between things, in terms of numbers – not just arithmetical matters, but everything, including human character and future potential. This premise assumes that the universe is ordered and that the order is mathematical. Moreover, the expression can be managed by the use of only the numbers 1 to 9, after which you are just re-using the same numbers. Numerology is always reducing compound numbers to single ones by left-to-right additions: 12 is $1 + 2 = 3$, and so on.

Most numerological fortune telling relies solely on the reduction to numbers of a name, a date, a keyword of a proposal for the future, or the like. With dates it is simple. October

Pythagoras, ancient Greek mathematician and philosopher

Mystical 'Pythagorean Wheel' of 19th-century numerology

12, 1971, reduces thus: 8 for October (the eighth month); 3 for
the date (12 = 1 + 2 = 3); 9 for the year (1 + 9 + 7 + 1 = 18 =
1 + 8 = 9). The total is 8 + 3 + 9 = 20 = 2 + 0 = 2. If that is an
important date to you, the traditional 'meanings' of the number
2 will tell you about the prospects for it.

If you do not like the prognostication, there are other
methods. Some numerologists offer meanings for compound
numbers, so you could interpret the number 20 for your date.
Or you could take the keywords representing the planned
activity and reduce them to numbers using a fixed letter-to-
number system. Numerology offers several: one obeys an old
Hebrew taboo and omits the number 9, supposedly the numer-
ical equivalent of the name of God. This system, and a less
reverent modern system using all the first nine numbers, are
shown on the pages following.

A widely used system of number-letter equivalents

1	2	3	4	5	6	7	8	9
A	B	C	D	E	F	G	H	I
J	K	L	M	N	O	P	Q	R
S	T	U	V	W	X	Y	Z	

Another common system, omitting the mystic number 9

1	2	3	4	5	6	7	8
A	B	C	D	E	U	O	F
I	K	G	M	H	V	Z	P
Q	R	L	T	N	W		
J		S			X		
Y							

What the Numbers Say

Most numerologists like to complicate their subject with cross-fertilizations from astrology, herbalism, colour and jewel symbolism and more. Space does not permit inclusion of these correspondences here; nor does it permit much explanation of why the Pythagoreans and later occultists thought of odd numbers as masculine and good, evens as feminine and bad. (Some of this notion grew from a basic occult concept that things in this world always come in opposites – day/night, sun/moon, male/female, yin/yang, etc.) Here we can merely offer encapsulated meanings ascribed to the numbers as in the many books of parlour-magic, tell-your-friends'-fortunes numerology.

1 is the One, the Creator, also the sun, and so displays leadership, dominance, power-seeking.

2 links with the moon and so with femininity: passive, changeable, even deceitful, but also inventive, sensitive and artistically inclined.

3 is also creative, spiritually so (the Trinity) but with sexual overtones too. Disciplined, proud, artistic.

4 is a complete number, and *earth*-oriented (the seasons, the directions). It forms a square, and its people are seen as square – dull, earthbound, potentially miserable, though sometimes with reformist, rebellious tendencies.

5 is also sexual, but not like 3 – not creative so much as pleasure-seeking, sensual (the five senses). A tendency to be impulsive, but resilient if baulked.

6 is a 'perfect' number, and so represents family love, domesticity, tidiness, reliability.

7 has major significance because so many groups are sevens or multiples (days of week, phases of moon, colours in the spectrum and more). So it indicates a love of philosophy, meditativeness, a leaning towards occultism, and is often thought of as a 'lucky' number.

8 sometimes echoes the problems of 4, but also stands for worldliness and possible material success.

9 is as sacred a number as 7, again because of all the groupings, especially the nine months of pregnancy. It is the ultimate in numerology, containing the highest qualities of courage, selflessness and brotherly love.

Numbers in Names

If John Citizen wants to know how numerology sees him, he turns his name into numbers by one of the systems shown. JOHN is $1+6+8+5=20$, or 2. CITIZEN is $3+9+2+9+8+5+5=41$, or 5. And $2+5=7$. His handbook of numerology will tell him what a 7 person is like, and what his future will be. He can also work out the number value of his birthdate, for comparison. For fun, he can add the number value of his birth year to the year itself: if born in 1939, he gets $1+9+3+9=22$, which, added to 1939, gives 1961, supposedly an important year for him. He can find out if he has the right job, by comparing the number value of its title to that of his name. He can find out if he is living in the right place, by working out the number value of his city's name. (The vowels in a city's name are said to denote its inner nature: those of wicked, feminine Paris add up to 2.) He can learn about the current year: 1973,

As an example, work out the numerology of Lincoln's name

for instance, becomes 2, suggesting a year for change, and a good one for artists – and the decade that began with 1970 is revealed by $1+9+7+0=17$, which is 8, which contains the revolutionary tendencies of 4, as all modern militants would agree.

John can also use the numbers to pick a wife, a horse in a race, a politician in an election, and a good day for any enterprise. If he does not like his results, there are alternative ways. If his name-number comes out unpleasantly, he can use his middle name too, or his initials. He can interpret the compound numbers of his names according to various systems, without reducing all numbers to final, one-figure numbers. Above all, he can rely on the loose, vague generalities of the handbooks, like those of any do-it-yourself fortune telling manuals, which remain purposefully flexible enough to be bent to suit any customer.

Or try using other presidents like Franklin D. Roosevelt

THE CASTING OF LOTS

'Lots' was originally an old Teutonic term for a collection of small objects used for divination. The process, which involved the casting or drawing of the lots, was and is called *sortilege*. Of course, sortilege today has become mainly a form of gambling – in the many forms of lottery, sweepstake, pools and so on – or a simple means of choosing someone to undertake a given job, etc., by drawing straws or tossing coins.

In the past, men might also have drawn straws or tossed the

Carved divining sticks from southern Africa, to be cast (like runes, dice and so on) to reveal the future

Right, sortilege in ancient Japan: a slip of paper drawn from a bowl containing a magically inscribed assortment

equivalent of coins to single out a particular individual – but this act would probably have been in the nature of a test, or 'ordeal', by which a tribe or community could spot an evil-doer among them. The gods, it was believed, would direct the short straw or whatever into the hands of the criminal. (Most primitive societies, though, used forms of torture instead of sortilege for the trial by ordeal; only the guilty, it was thought, would suffer pain.) Also, the *drawing* of lots – which has now degenerated to merely the drawing of the winning number in something like the Irish Sweepstakes – might provide a simple yes-or-no answer to some query about the future: will the crops be abundant? Will we win the war? Will I have many sons?

In ancient Japan one might place magically inscribed slips of paper into a container and draw one for an omen referring to an enterprise. It would be less simple than a yes or no, but still it would not require much interpretation. In western antiquity, such slips of paper might have contained meaningful fragments of a sacred book (there is a tie-up here with 'bibliomancy', for which see

Runic letters carved on Sweden's ancient Björkentorpstone

92

later), and the drawing might be done by a stranger accosted for that purpose. At other times the bits of paper might be spilled from the container, to take the omen from which emerged first, or which landed right side up. This is *casting lots* – for which almost any kind of object has been used, though mainly sticks, stones and sacred bones.

Casting the Runes

The runes were the stark, strange characters of the alphabet used by the Germanic and Nordic peoples from about the second or third century A.D. They were considered to be not only containers of communication, like any writing, but of a most potent magic. The myth says that Odin, king of the gods, underwent great torment (including the loss of an eye) to gain power over the runes, from which came his own divine power. So Teutonic magicians carved the runes to work their magic – believing them able to rule the weather, defeat enemies, even to wake the dead.

One common technique required the carving of runes onto small blocks of special wood, like beech, which would be scattered or 'cast' on a white cloth. The diviner might interpret the meaning of the pattern they made, the interrelationships, or he might pick them up one at a time, at random, and read the omens that way. Tacitus, the Roman historian, says that the pagan Germans would cut a bough from a fruit tree, cut it into small pieces and mark them, scatter them on a cloth, then pick them up three at a time for interpreting. The markings would undoubtedly have been runic.

Sticks marked with special letters or magical signs (not runes but similar) have been found among the leavings of ancient Alpine peoples, and were probably used in divination. Marked magic sticks are fairly widely used by diviners, in many lands. In ancient Greece, specially marked wooden counters went into an urn, to be cast or drawn. The Romans wrote the letters of their alphabet on small bits of wood, then cast them and read the words or non-words made by their scattering. Carved flat 'tablets' of wood are used by magicians in many African tribes, in Rhodesia, the Transvaal and elsewhere. Many North American Indians divined by casting a handful of specially marked sacred arrows. The use of arrows, called 'belomancy', goes back to ancient Babylon – and was carried on somewhat later by the Arabs, who used arrows marked with oracular statements which they *drew* from a container to answer questions or give omens.

Throwing Stones

Still on the subject of sortilege, diviners may well use small stones or pebbles as their lots, instead of sticks or small pieces of wood. Divination by casting a handful of pebbles is called 'pessomancy', and is as widespread as any form of casting lots. The Greeks who, as mentioned before, placed small wooden counters into an urn before spilling them and reading omens in the scatter, often substituted appropriately marked pebbles. The Arabs (and others) have often preferred to spill out the special stones into a compact heap, and then draw carefully, at random, one stone at a time, reading the omens as they come. This method is called 'psephomancy', from the Greek for pebble – which is related to the Greek word for a vote; hence the modern art of *psephology*, the analysis (and sometimes prediction, but not by casting stones) of elections.

Ancient dice: astragals and other Graeco-Roman variations

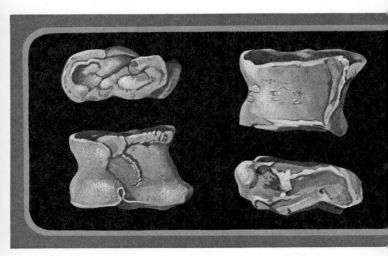

With stones, of course, special markings may not be necessary as long as the pebbles differ sufficiently from one another. In most cases, with these forms of sortilege, no one has imposed onto them the standardized meanings of other kinds of fortune telling. The diviner knows the omens to be found in the stones, but of course they are usually kept secret, so that the pessomancy market remains cornered. The many African tribes where the witchdoctors had bagsful of 'wise stones' – for instance, in the Transvaal, or among the Nandi of East Africa – are traditionally conscious of the secrecy of this knowledge.

Celtic peoples have a traditional form of divination that uses stones in a simple, 'singling-out' form of sortilege, though with a strong element of mystery and magic. In Scotland the custom was to place a circle of stones, each marked by one of the participants, around a bonfire on Halloween. The next morning, if any stone had moved from its place, the owner would be doomed to die in the ensuing year. A Welsh variant, found also in Brittany, required the participants to throw their stones *into* the fire on Midsummer night; if any stone had mysteriously vanished from the ashes, next morning, it was again a death omen.

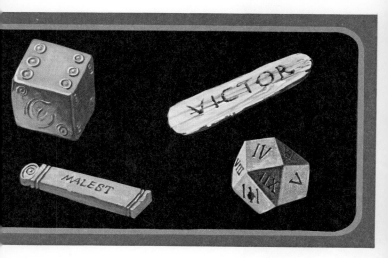

An African witch doctor with his divinatory 'wise stones'

Prophetic Bones

The fateful objects used in the casting of lots might well be bits of shell, bark, beads, or anything. The oracular Chinese book called *I Ching* demands the throwing of yarrow stalks in a blend of bibliomancy and sortilege. The most popular objects through the ages, aside from sticks and stones, have been bones.

They might be any small fragments of an animal's skeleton, with special markings. South African tribes used flat pieces of bone like the wooden tablets mentioned before; the bones were used, among other things, to divine what spirit was causing an illness and what offerings would appease it. Otherwise, ancient diviners have preferred small bones like the vertebrae – or, most commonly, the ankle bones of sheep which classical antiquity called *astragals*. Of course Greece and Rome also possessed other prophetic bones, including the flat kind with different marks on each side, to be tossed like coins for yes-or-no answers about the future. The four-sided astragals were used in many

Early AmerIndian bone dice

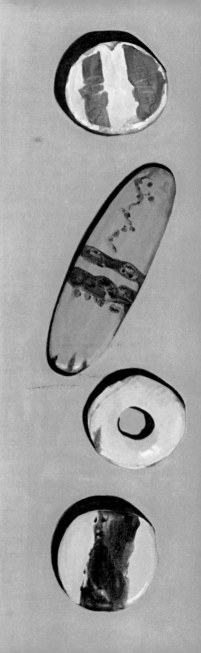

games (for gambling or mere pleasure), and so tended to be more plentiful than other kinds of bones. These bones were the direct ancestors of our dice (which slang still terms 'the bones'): just as the ancient games have given way to modern dice games, so astragalomancy and other kinds of 'cleromancy' (sortilege by casting small objects) have given way to plain fortune telling by throwing dice.

Before looking at that subject, we might mention another use of prophetic bones, called 'scapulomancy', that uses the shoulderblade of, usually, a sheep. Moslem diviners and others in the past used the shoulderblades of sacrificial animals, and read the lines and marks on them for messages from the gods. The Scots looked to such bones for the future, and one folktale refers to a soldier predicting from the bone the outcome of Culloden. In some traditions the bone should be heated until divinatory cracks appear: the Eskimo, heating a seal's shoulderblade, see good hunting in a long transverse crack.

More primitive bone or wood dice

A Roll of the Dice

Fortune telling by dice may not be as widely popular as that which uses cards, but is sufficiently up to date to have become standardized in handbooks of ready-made interpretations, a far cry from the shaman studying his stones or magic bones.

At its simplest, dice divination requires you to throw two dice within a circle to answer questions. (Throwing within a circle seems standard practice with dice; magic words or gestures are optional.) The questions tend to be along the lines of 'Will my wish come true?' or 'Does he/she love me?' or 'Will I be rich?' or even 'Will I be found out?' The answers are as loose and accommodatingly flexible as the questions are puerile. Rolling 7 means 'Yes, if you rely on yourself'; 11 is 'Take a chance' but 5 is 'No, unless you are cautious'. Sometimes you can roll the two dice twice, adding the scores, so the answers go up to 24.

Other systems attach a meaning to every number possible from three dice, briefly as follows: 3 means the unexpected; 4, unpleasantness; 5, a wish coming true; 6, a loss; 7, business setbacks; 8, outside influences; 9, marriage; 10, birth; 11, a parting; 12, good news; 13, sorrow; 14, a helpful friend; 15, take care; 16, travel; 17, a change of plans; and 18 is success.

If one die rolls out of the circle, it foretells upset plans; two out mean a quarrel, three mean a wish coming true. The circle could also be divided into twelve segments, each with a specific association to an area of life, thus: next year; money; travel; the home; present occupations; health; marriage; death; mental state; job; friends; enemies. Matters are complicated when each segment must be interpreted according to the number of dice, and spots shown, that fall within it. Manuals give accounts, but of a parlour-game level.

Closely related to dice divination is the sort that uses dominoes – those 28 oblong tablets of wood or ivory, spotted like the sides of dice. Most simply, you shuffle the pieces face down and draw, turning to standard interpretations for the meanings. The double six is excellent luck; the six–blank advises caution; the five–one hints at a love affair; four–two means a robbery; double three means a marriage; one–blank is good news; double blank means disaster.

THE DEVIL'S PICTURE BOOK

Though he may never play bridge or poker, a person concerned with magic – whether high adept or Sunday dabbler – will never be without his pack of cards. They will not be the cards we immediately think of; they will be the predecessors of our modern pack, the mystic and beautiful Tarot cards, in which, as one commentator has breathlessly put it, 'destiny is reflected

LE MAT

L'IMPERATRICE

L'EMPEREUR

as in a mirror with multiple facets'. Cards probably first came into the western world from the Arabs, and the Tarot was fairly well known by the 14th century, when it was used for games as well as divination. By the 15th, early forms of our 52-card pack had come into being, mainly for games, and the Tarot had gone firmly into the hands of the occultists. So it came to be known as the 'devil's picture book' – a phrase sometimes foolishly applied by anti-gambling puritans to the rather less pictorial modern pack.

The usual Tarot pack contains 78 cards. It is made up of four suits with fourteen cards each, because there are *four* court cards in each – King, Queen, Knight and Knave. These court cards form the Minor Arcana, from which some divination can be managed. The real power is lodged in the 22 'trump' cards of the Major Arcana, with their splendid pictorial figures that are said to contain symbolically all occult mystery. These are numbered differently in different systems; the following is a common system, and also gives a key word or two indicating the usual associations.

Six cards from the trumps or 'Major Arcana' of an old French Tarot pack, still in use today. Illustrations differ from pack to pack, but the 22 subjects remain the same

1, Juggler (choice, freedom). 2, High Priestess (wisdom, perhaps occult). 3, Empress (fertility). 4, Emperor (protective power). 5, Pope (tradition, society). 6, Lovers (passion, marriage). 7, Chariot (travel, success). 8, Justice (abstractly representing itself). 9, Hermit (wisdom). 10, Wheel of Fortune (good luck). 11, Strength (itself). 12, Hanged Man (prudence, but daring too). 13, Death (itself). 14, Temperance (itself). 15, Devil (aggression, sex). 16, Falling Tower (ruin). 17, Star (hope). 18, Moon (creativity, irrationality). 19, Sun (light,

XI

LA FORCE

XIIII

TEMPERANCE

XVII

L'ETOILE

reason). 20, Judgment (the will). 21, World (travel, achievement). Then the usually unnumbered Fool, taken to be man as he truly is, the aspirations and folly of human nature.

Six more cards of the Major Arcana. Note the introduction of astrological tie-ups, as in the crab symbol (Cancer) on the moon card — as well as other extra symbolic images

XVIII

LA LUNE

XVIIII

LE SOLEIL

XX

LE JUGEMENT

Manipulating the Tarot

No one should think that the foregoing is even an approximation of the symbolism in the Major Arcana. Things grow even more complicated as regards their use in divination. There are nearly as many usages as users: some use the whole pack, others use parts, they shuffle in special ways and lay out the cards in special ways. One common layout resembles that shown on page 105. It forms three vertical 'pillars' standing for (left to right) discipline, harmony and love. The horizontal rows have meanings too: the top three packs are, left to right, concerned with knowledge, idealism and wisdom. Thus interpretation can begin with the cards face down. Turned up, the cards in each pack are interpreted according to their tangled symbolism and also their inter-relations, which are vitally important – as it is if a card is upside down, which reverses its usual meaning. Obviously it is not something that can be readily fitted into a nutshell, or picked up by amateurs without lengthy study and experience.

Some fortune tellers clearly feel the same, for they prefer to use only the Minor Arcana – still colourfully pictorial but by no means so intricate. The four suits of the Tarot are called Swords (spades), Cups (hearts), Wands (clubs) and Coins or Pentacles (diamonds). Their associations, respectively, are with sadness, happiness, news and money. One system ascribes meanings as follows to the four court cards (King, Queen, Knave, Knight): of Swords, a bad man or a judge; a bad woman or a widow; a deceiver; a soldier. Of Cups: a fair and powerful man; a fair woman; a true knave or rogue; a fair and worthy young man. Of Wands: a dark man, perhaps dangerous; a dark woman; a dark youth, perhaps a wastrel; a lazy person. Of Coins: a good, strict man; a good strict woman; good news; discord and departure.

Different sources offer different meanings. Also, non-court cards have their meanings: the eight of Swords means ill health and bad news; the ten of Cups means success; the nine of Coins means a lasting wealth, whereas the six means a calamitous financial loss; the seven of Wands means progress achieved towards a goal; and so on.

Cards of the Modern Pack

The meanings generally assigned to the ordinary, non-court cards of the Tarot have in many cases devolved onto the ordinary cards of the modern pack – though of course its divinatory uses are more simple than the Tarot's. Individual cards have their special meanings (varying from one manual to another) and the suits too have special associations. Hearts link with love and domesticity; Spades with sorrow and loss; Diamonds with society and one's work, sometimes money; Clubs with money, sometimes travel, and ambition.

The Ace of Hearts concerns happiness in love; the King, a fair aristocratic man; Queen, a fair woman; Jack, a young man or lover; 10, love; 9, success; 8, a visitor; 7, good news; 6, unexpected luck; 5, unexpected money; 4, a change; 3, enjoyment; 2, friendship.

The Ace of Spades is popularly thought to be the death card but often means merely legal trouble; King, a strong man, army officer or judge; Queen, a seductive woman; Jack, a dark young man; 10, worry, loss; 9, sorrow, the true card of death; 8, disappointment; 7, a warning; 6, change in fortune; 5, a funeral; 4, peace; 3, parting; 2, deceit.

The Ace of Diamonds can mean messages or a betrothal; King, a strong man of affairs, wealthy; Queen, a fair woman, sophisticated; Jack, a pleasant young man, or a letter; 10, money or a journey; 9, a new start; 8, unexpected money; 7, a gift; 6, reconciliation; 5, a meeting; 4, inheritance; 3, social activity; 2, a warning.

The Ace of Clubs indicates an important achievement; the King, a dark man, politician or statesman; Queen, a dark woman of strong character; Jack, an extravagant young man; 10, riches or travel; 9, romance; 8, opposition; 7, money; 6, good news; 5, a threat; 4, enjoyment; 3, friendliness; 2, new developments.

These standard meanings can be extracted at a reading by simply shuffling the pack, cutting it into three sections, and turning up the top card of each. Of course there are more complex layouts, to be looked at next; in all of these, combinations of cards can alter or reinforce meanings.

The 'Tree of Life' layout for reading the Tarot pack

More Modern Cartomancy

Among the combinations of cards to watch for, pairs have special meanings – and whatever a pair means, a three or four of that card means the same thing only more extremely. A pair of aces means success, three mean considerable success, four mean superlative success. So kings mean good business; queens, beware of slander; jacks, an argument; tens, money coming; nines, good fortune, and so on. As examples of other linkings, the ace and eight of spades mean disaster, ace of diamonds and nine of spades mean ill health, ace and seven of diamonds warns of a major quarrel.

Cards also combine in special layouts, like that on page 105, a common Tarot pattern also used in ordinary cartomancy. Each of the ten packs (seven cards in each if the Tarot is used) refers to an area of life, and the meanings of individual cards within each are related to those areas. Number 1 refers to God and the spirit; 2 to paternity; 3 to maternity; 4 to compassion; 5 to strength; 6 to sacrifice; 7 to love; 8 to the arts and sciences; 9 to health; 10 to general worldliness. Also, aside from forming vertical 'pillars' as mentioned before, they form triangles meaning (top to bottom) Spirit, Reason, Intellect.

Less complicated, because less directly linked with Tarot mysticism, is the layout on page 107. The central card is a court card 'resembling' the subject of the reading (the King of Clubs, say, if the subject is a mature dark man). The nine packs, with three cards each, refer to specific areas of the subject's concern. Pack 1 refers to current concerns above the subject – i.e. imposing on him. Pack 2, below him, refers to matters in his control. Pack 3 is the past, behind him; 4 is the immediate future, in front of him. Pack 5 is domestic matters; 6, hopes and fears; 7, the unexpected; 8, expectations; 9, certainties for the future.

Basil Ivan Rakoczi, an expert on gypsy fortune telling, calls this layout the Wheel of Fortune. The reading simply involves turning up the cards of each pack, in order, interpreting them singly but also building up an overall pattern reflecting the pattern of the subject's life.

A common layout for reading the modern pack, showing the order in which the cards are to be picked up

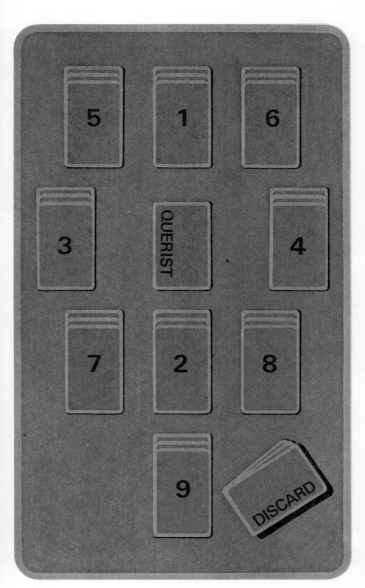

GEOMANCY

As the name implies, geomancy means divination by means of the earth, which may seem a fairly unwieldy implement. Its ancient practice in fact required the use not of the planet but of portions of *soil* – and, sometimes, pebbles, twigs, seeds and the like which were considered 'earthy' because they were to be found on the ground. Thus there is an obvious possible confusion with forms of sortilege that use sticks or stones – all the more so because geomancy, whatever material is employed, depends like sortilege on finding 'meaningful' patterns in random marks or shapes.

Its special nature comes principally from its use, and the refinement of its principles, by the high occult masters of the ancient Arabs, who undoubtedly inherited the system from even more ancient experts. The geomantic tradition says that one should cast a handful of earth (or sand, or fine dust) onto some smooth surface like a marble tabletop, and look to the figures it makes. Another technique is of more interest to us today, for it has given rise to an entirely up-to-date system still in use. In this special technique the Arabs would make a smooth surface of fine earth or sand, and the diviner would make random marks in it with an implement. At its simplest, the seer would be prodding with a stick at a patch of ground smoothed by hand. More sophisticatedly, he would use a special tray with a thin spreading of white sand, and perhaps a slim ivory wand.

The wand is said to move almost of itself, as in spiritualists' 'automatic writing'. It may inscribe letters ('y' for yes, 'n' for no, persons' initials), numbers or whole words. Or it might simply make obscure marks, though some of these have been predictably systematized: long lines mean travel, short ones mean visitors, circles mean weddings, upright triangles mean success, a cross means bad news or a death but several crosses can be favourable, a clearly made square can also be favourable, portending happiness, and so on.

Arab geomancy: the diviner is blindfolded as he inscribes marks at random on the smoothed surface of the ground, to be interpreted as a prophecy for his client

Pen and Paper

Modern geomancers may lack white sand, so will instead make their random marks with a pen or pencil on paper. In a most common technique, the diviner (exercising minimal control) lets the pencil make an indeterminate number of points from right to left, in a line – then makes three more such lines, and counts the points. If a line holds an even number, it is represented by two dots; if uneven, one dot. Now he repeats the process, of forming four lines of points, three times. The result is four *shapes* made out of dots – one or another of the standard shapes shown below.

Four of the shapes are called 'Mothers'. By shifting some dots within each, according to special rules, you get the four shapes called 'Daughters', then four 'Nephews', two 'Witnesses' and one 'Judge'. In most cases a shape's meaning alters if it functions as Mother or Witness or whatever; also, meanings are read in terms of astrological houses, the shapes being

The shapes of pen-and-paper geomancy and their names

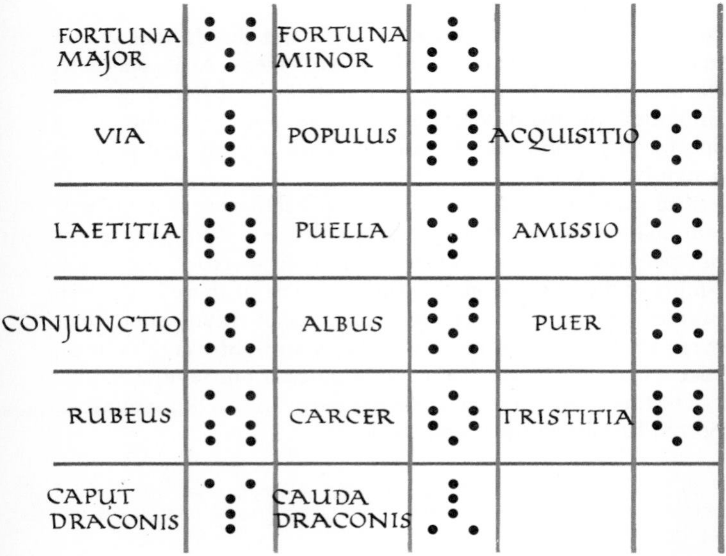

FORTUNA MAJOR	• •	FORTUNA MINOR	• •		
	•		• •		
VIA	•	POPULUS	• •	ACQUISITIO	• •
	•		• •		•
	•		• •		•
	•		• •		•
LAETITIA	• •	PUELLA	•	AMISSIO	• •
	•		•		• •
	•		• •		•
CONJUNCTIO	• •	ALBUS	•	PUER	•
	•		• •		• •
	• •		• •		• •
RUBEUS	•	CARCER	• •	TRISTITIA	• •
	• •		•		• •
	• •		• •		•
CAPUT DRACONIS	• •	CAUDA DRACONIS	•		
	•		• •		

interrelated by means of various complex systems. Agrippa says that Fortune Major means, obviously, great good fortune, while Carcer means constraint, Tristitia sadness and so on. The occultist Franz Hartmann, writing in 1913, feels that geomancy works best answering specific questions: he offers 16 sample questions (about long life, health, wealth, success, that sort of thing) and 2048 sample answers from different shapes in different houses.

If these marks on paper seem to have come too far from the ancient divinatory use of earth, you can move back towards those usages by a sortileginous method that is still, with variations, to be found today in gypsy and other traditions. You may simply take a handful of twigs – or matches if you prefer – and cast them on a smooth surface. All high-sounding ritual, Fortunae Major and so on, vanishes; plain rote interpretation operates, as in the examples shown.

Right, a truly random and yet do-it-yourself form of geomancy: 'prophetic' shapes that might be made by tossing matches on any smooth surface

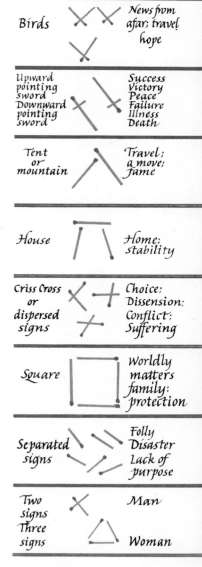

Birds		News from afar; travel hope
Upward pointing sword Downward pointing sword		Success Victory Peace Failure Illness Death
Tent or mountain		Travel; a move; fame
House		Home; stability
Criss Cross or dispersed signs		Choice; Dissension; Conflict; Suffering
Square		Worldly matters family; protection
Separated signs		Folly Disaster Lack of purpose
Two signs Three signs		Man Woman

HYDROMANCY

Just as geomancy can overlap with sortilege, in some forms, so hydromancy – divination by means of water – can overlap with crystal gazing. Many sorts of fortune telling can be interconnected in this way. Anyway, crystal gazing is or once was a sub-branch of a broader form of divination that used any reflecting surface – of which, in antiquity, water was the most important. If the crystal has now virtually taken over the entire field, it is nonetheless true that water-gazing, so to speak, once held pride of place (though see the discussion of mirrors, later).

The ancients prognosticated by gazing for visions into water in a variety of ways: in a cup or bowl, using the surface of the water like a mirror (such as Joseph's divining cup, mentioned in Genesis XLIV; or in a round or bulbous glass container (called 'gastronomancy' because of the belly shape); or in natural water, pools or springs or even rivers. Of course the containers might often have held wine, ink or other fluids; it was all hydromancy, for it was the reflecting liquidity that mattered. Also, the active seeing (as with the crystal, in past centuries) would sometimes be done by a virgin child, most usually a boy, who would perceive the images that the magician would interpret.

The ancient Babylonians apparently preferred using liquid in special magic bowls; their inheritors in the Middle East, even in modern times, are said still to use this method. The Babylonians also read futures in the state and appearance of rivers, where they saw manifestations of one of their major deities, a water god. Not surprisingly, the ancient Egyptians also divined from the Nile (that is, the Nile god, Hapi), for the river was too important to their survival to be left out of their supernatural thinking. The Greeks preferred pools or sacred springs, but also used containers indoors.

The Uses of Water

When the Greeks went to a poolside to divine, they usually merely dropped pebbles into the water and took omens from

A favourite form of hydromancy in ancient Greece – dropping stones into a clear pool and reading omens in the ripples the size, speed, number and so on of ripples. Later times added a refinement: the magician dropped, in order, a round stone, a triangular one and a cubical one. Ripples could also be important when made by the wind, but here we trespass on aeromancy. Most of the elaborations of ripple interpretation have since vanished into obscurity; a fairly modern book of magic offers the ultra-simple notion that an odd number of ripples means good fortune or a favourable reply to a query, an even number means the opposite.

At Kolophon, a sacred spring would inspire one who drank from it, making him both insane and a prophet (the two were often considered interchangeable); other oracles, even the Delphic, used holy spring water to reinforce their power. Some wells or springs in Greece were semi-magical healers,

From ancient Babylon to modern Europe and the Middle East diviners will sometimes seek the future by gazing into liquid in a sacred bowl, as if into a crystal ball

or provided (if one slept near them) medically divinatory dreams. At Amorgos, omens were taken from bits of flotsam – dust, leaves, insects, whatever – on the surface of a cup of water drawn from a holy well. At Patrai and elsewhere diviners lowered a mirror into a spring and looked into it for prophetic visions (but see mirrors); in Lykia and Tainaron sacred springs themselves showed such images (and the process is called pegomancy).

The Greeks of course believed that the gods used the water to provide a prophetic message. The Romans shared the idea: one legend tells of a magic fountain in which Hadrian saw a prediction that he would be emperor. Afterwards, to forestall anyone replacing him because of similar encouragement, he had the fountain blocked up.

Today, hydromancy has degenerated into silly sortilege-type usages, such as that which tells you to write various courses of action on bits of paper and cover them with water in a bowl. The 'recommended' course will be on the paper that first rises to the surface.

AEROMANCY

The foregoing is not at all an exhaustive account of the methods of fortune telling that use water, simply because so many forms utilize water as a secondary material, the primary place going to such things as mirrors, rings, jewels and the like (some to be looked at later). Aeromancy – divination by means of the air and its movements, and by aspects of the sky – should potentially be as broad in scope. As it happens this art has grown even more obscure than its watery cousin. Though there are a few minor uses of winds and so on in fortune telling still, the aeromancy of ancient times seems to have declined now into simple weather lore.

In the past, weather or sky divination was taken to a high and complex art by the Etruscans. One of their principal deities was Tin, or Tinia, god of fire and thunder, hurler of lightning at the earth. The Etruscan priests, conscious of their god and other portents of the sky, built their temples on hilltops like observatories, concerned themselves with the strength and duration of lightning but especially with the direction from which thunder rolled (for these purposes they considered the sky to have sixteen distinct areas). Later, in Roman times, the philosopher-playwright Seneca was among those who thought that portents might be read in thunder; and an echo of this ancient view of thunder still remains in current superstitions, among them the belief that thunder from the east portends bloodshed of some sort during the year, that thunder in winter foreshadows many deaths in summer or the specific death of a great man – or, less morbidly, prolonged good weather in the summer to come.

Winds, too, can be comparable omens: beliefs going back centuries say that a high wind on Christmas night means the death of kings in the year to come. And the death of a monarch in war is heralded by a stormy wind on Twelfth Night. Obviously storms and lightning and high winds, things which would have unnerved our primitive forebears, would be reflected as evil omens in later folk beliefs.

The ancient Etruscan god of thunder, fire and the sky, Tin or Tinia, who dominated their divinatory processes

Written on the Wind

Non-turbulent skies also found their uses in ancient and now mostly forgotten aeromantic procedures. Apparently the shapes of clouds were often interpreted as were those other dramatic shapes of fire, smoke and so on. A 19th-century French writer alludes to an even more obscure form of aeromancy in which a black magician's spells caused a demon to project images of the future onto the clouds, like (as he put it) 'a magic lantern'.

Omens from the sky, stormy or otherwise, do not form the whole of aeromancy. Diviners can also use the movements of air in a slightly less random, 'channelled' way. Ripples on water formed important processes in hydromancy, as noted before; but when those ripples were formed by the passage of a breeze over a special bowl of water that is *uncovered* at an auspicious moment (usually astrologically determined), the process can be seen more as aeromancy. In fact it was a common aeromantic method, in the ancient world. Diviners of antiquity are also said to have taken omens from sounds created by the wind, which would blow – again in a kind of controlled randomness – on special arrangements of musical instruments, or bells, or metal objects hung on trees to clang and rattle together. A few authorities have seen something of this practice in references to Joan of Arc hearing prophetic voices in the sound of church bells.

With these techniques we have come a long way from omens taken from the weather, that primitive meteorology which has if nothing else the grandeur of the heavens to recommend it. Coming even further from the near-sublime to the very near-ridiculous, there is a 20th-century form of aeromancy that is at the same time a form of sortilege, or drawing of lots. This degenerate technique uses a man-made flow of air. As in the previously described modern form of hydromancy, the diviner writes various courses of action, or alternative answers to a question, on bits of paper and places them face down on a table. He then turns on an electric *fan* and directs it at the papers; the first to be blown face up, or off the table, provides the oracle.

American Plains Indians read omens in their immense skies

BIBLIOMANCY

Divination by means of a book is more or less another form of sortilege, in the drawing of lots sense. It is also a desperately simple way of obtaining a 'sign', which explains its continuing popularity. The basic technique is simply to allow a book to fall open at random, and to take the omen from the first words on which your eyes rest. Or you can open the book at random and jab the page with a pin, if you don't mind mutilating your books. The Bible tends to be used most, these days as in the past; even St. Augustine admitted that he had recourse to this form of divination, and in the sixth century A.D. the church fathers found it so widespread that they issued edicts against it. Some practitioners, instead of using the whole Bible, identify the 31 verses of the last chapter of Proverbs with the days of a particular month, and so can look up a daily omen if they wish one.

In antiquity, books by various major poets were used, like the Greek epics of Homer or the Persian poems of Hafiz (and for the latter a knife would be inserted at random between pages, and the omen found at the top of the right-hand page thus indicated). The works of the Roman poet Virgil came in for more use than anyone's, even down to the Middle Ages and later, when such bibliomancy was called 'Virgilian Lots'. The medieval authorities often ascribed unlikely legends of magical and mystical power to Virgil: remember for instance that he is the dreamer's guide through hell in Dante's *Inferno*. In the 17th century Charles I reportedly used Virgil's *Aeneid* in bibliomancy and got (from Book IV) an unsettling but apt reference to rebels and regicide.

The Bible is often used with a key in the process called 'cleidomancy': the key is bound within the book (often in the Psalms) and hung by a thread from the diviner's finger or that of an innocent child. The book will supposedly spin, or fall, when the diviner utters the right answer to the question under consideration.

The poet Dante gazing at a book. His use of the Roman poet Virgil as a spiritual guide echoes the mediaeval view of Virgil as a mage, and the use of his poems in bibliomancy

The *I Ching*

The Chinese 'Book of Changes', at least 2000 years old and said to be the oldest existing book in the world, is a container of high and symbolic wisdom, recognized as such not only by the Chinese. Confucius wished he had 50 years to study it, would-be civil servants in Imperial China had it on their examination reading list, Japanese samurai learned approaches to combat based on some of its precepts. In later times its oracular or divinatory uses have been much emphasized, but its reputation as a conveyor of wisdom is not diminished, even in the west – especially since C. G. Jung used its example to refine his theory of 'synchronicity'. (That, to oversimplify wildly, suggests that two events can be meaningfully and symbolically related though there is no cause-and-effect connection between them.)

In ordinary low-brow fortune telling the *I Ching* utilizes sortilege: you cast lots, their pattern provides you with a special symbol or figure, and you look that up in the book for your oracle. The proper Chinese method demands the casting of yarrow stalks, but modern western users prefer to throw three coins. The coins are usually thrown six times, to give the six lines of the desired 'hexagram' (see illustration). The predominance of heads or tails in each throw gives an unbroken or broken line (positive or negative, the traditional yin-yang Chinese awareness of the opposing qualities in man and the universe).

The seeker then looks up his hexagram in the book. There are 64 possible hexagrams; for each there is a fairly clear-cut oracular pronouncement. With it there is also much discussion and elaboration (said to be Confucian) of the hexagram's symbolism, of that inherent in each line, and of other related matters. This extension of the oracle will usually be quite cryptic, or at least susceptible of considerable interpretation – for which many serious users turn to a teacher or master. The most popular translation in the west, by Richard Wilhelm, fills two fat volumes in its English version, which is a great deal of compact, difficult material. Students say that as a source of ancient inspiration it deserves more study, and more respect, than comes with its use for merely telling one's fortune.

Some of the more important 'hexagrams', made up of either broken or unbroken lines, that can be obtained when using the *I Ching* – with their general meanings encapsulated

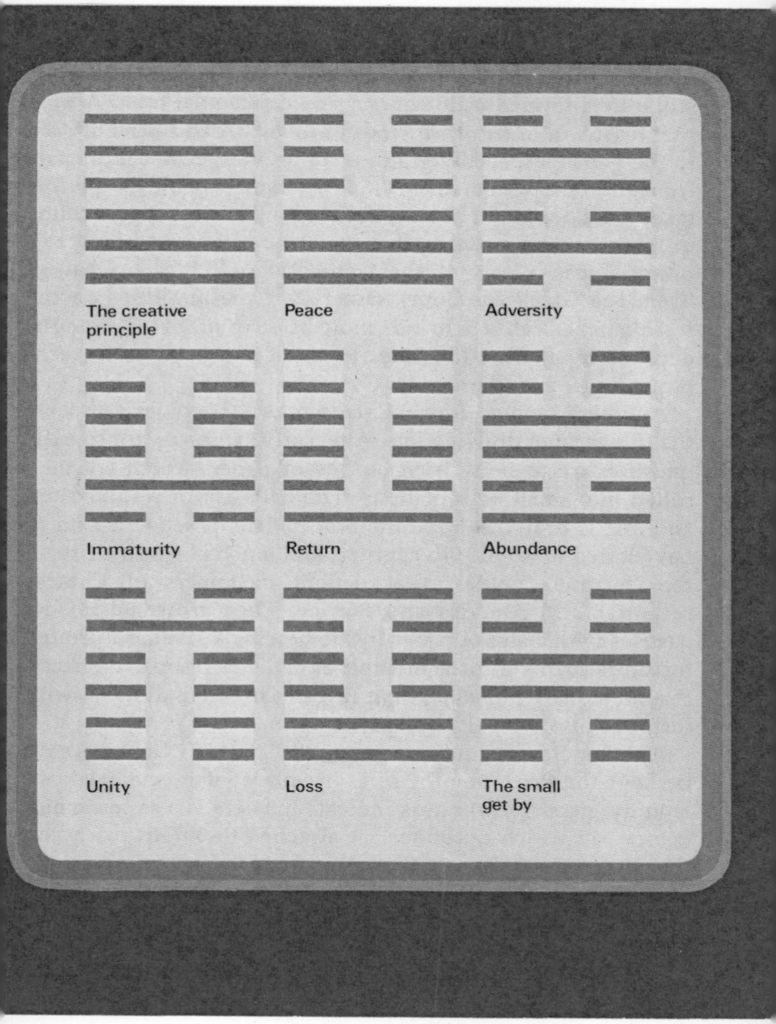

The creative
principle

Peace

Adversity

Immaturity

Return

Abundance

Unity

Loss

The small
get by

MINOR MANTIC ARTS

Edible Fortunes

The animal entrails used in haruspicy, discussed earlier, usually came from beasts that had been sacrificed to the gods. Often, in ancient Greece and other civilizations, other portions of the sacrificed animal were burnt, to be the god's share, while still others formed main courses at a ceremonial feast. Also at that feast would be other kinds of food that had been offered to the gods – especially grain, or flour, or special cakes made from the flour. From these, too, divination could be performed. The flour might be cast, like the sand or dust of geomancy, to form random patterns that could be interpreted, and this practice was a part of the technique called 'aleuromancy' (from the Greek for flour). Otherwise, the markings on the freshly baked cakes or bread would be scrutinized for portents, decoded by another intricate system of meanings in the technique known as 'crithomancy'.

Another common form of aleuromancy involves a process that is a form of drawing lots. Alternative answers to a specific question are to be written on bits of paper, which are then rolled into small balls of flour. The balls are then mixed up, and one is drawn to give the oracle. This practice is said to have lasted up to the 9th century, and much of it still exists in the 'fortune cookies' that delight customers of Chinese restaurants in America and Europe. They are small hollow pastries with a slip of paper inside bearing a standard printed fortune – rather like the inedible but still traditional 'crackers' that are noisily pulled apart at British Christmas dinners, with fortunes inside on slips of paper.

Another British tradition required 'Twelfth Night cake' to be kept for three months in a dry place; if it remained not mouldy, good fortune was indicated. There is also 'cromniomancy', in which questions are attached to onions placed on the altar on Christmas Eve; the first to sprout gives the oracular answer. But some people prefer to plant their onions in their gardens, for the same result.

A typical Chinese fortune cookie, with some of the over-generalised sort of 'prophecies' obtainable from them

In the Balance

Objects suspended or balanced, to swing free as pointers, crop up in many common forms of fortune telling – including the form of bibliomancy mentioned before using a key and a Bible. A variation of that suspends only a key on a thread from a virgin's third finger, while a verse of Psalms is spoken; if the key spins, the omen is good. Today, needles hung horizontally from thread form a popular parlour-game divination. Perhaps it is that revolutions leftwards mean no, rightwards yes; or perhaps the needle predicts one's romantic future, or the number of children a girl will have, by revolving or moving sideways or remaining still while suspended over the wrist or sometimes over the heart.

Rings may be used as well: in ancient times 'dactylomancy' concerned special rings worn in connection with the planets, providing fortunes by a means now obscure, but today rings on threads may be used as pointers in a circle of the alphabet rather like the ouija board. Or the ring can be dangled into a container of water, and if it moves to strike the right side, the omen is good (or it means 'yes', to your question); the left side is of course the opposite. It is said that the ring can be hung from a hair of the diviner's head, for increased efficiency, and that it should preferably be a wedding band. Rings on silken threads were used as pendulums over maps by German wives during World War II, to divine their husbands' whereabouts; this is dactylomancy become radiesthesia, for which see earlier.

As for balancing acts, some ancient peoples would stand an axe on its head and dance round it till it fell; and if it fell on the right it was a good omen, or an affirmative answer. Sometimes this 'axinomancy' was used to point to a thief, or to buried treasure. 'Coscinomancy', popular in antiquity and also in the Middle Ages, used a sieve held in the air by tongs which were kept shut by two person's middle fingers. The diviner recited the names of suspects in a crime, or certain possible answers to a question, and the sieve drops at the correct utterance without volition on the part of the holder.

Divining an answer to a question by suspending a gold wedding ring on a thread over a bowl of water

Up in Flames

Earth, air and water have been seen in their mantic roles, so it will be no surprise that the remaining one of the ancient four elements, fire, finds its way into divination in pyromancy. The flames of sacrificial rites were especially important: Roman diviners among others watched the fire that rose when the offerings were burnt, and the omen was good if the offerings caught fire quickly and burnt brightly, with a clear flame not too red, little smoke, and no crackling noises. For the ancients too, resin or pitch tossed onto a fire should blaze up immediately for a good sign, as should pounded peas; laurel branches that crackled on a fire also predicted good fortune.

Other pyromantic divination employed the flame of a torch: if it formed one point, or three, good luck was indicated, but two points were unfortunate. If the flame bent, it foretold sickness; if it went out suddenly, disaster. Similar prognostications were made with the flame of a lamp, in 'lampadomancy'. 'Lychnomancy' used three fine wax candles: a left-to-right wavering of their flames meant travel; spiralling foretold enemies' plots; a rising and falling meant danger; one candle burning brighter than the others meant success; sparks warned of the need for caution; a bright point on the wick's end meant good fortune; one candle inexplicably going out spelled calamity.

Of other lesser forms that used fire, there was the interesting 'sideromancy', tossing an odd number of straws onto red-hot iron and interpreting their curling, writhing motions as they burn. Apollonius of Tyana alluded once to pyromantic use of the sun's corona, by gazing into it for visions, but the method is not recommended to anyone who values his retinas. Somewhat safer is the old practice of looking for crystal-ball-type visions in a domestic fire, as found among pagan Nordic tribes and in later European folklore. The sight of a mountain would mean success, a calm sea meant a peaceful life, an eagle was a warning, a sword meant danger, a fountain meant happiness, wings indicated travel, and so on.

Ancient Nordic diviners gather round a great fire (perhaps sacrificial) to read the future in the extent, shape, movement and other qualities of the flames

Insubstantial Fortunes

Many of the forms of pyromancy shade naturally into the almost equally popular (in past centuries) technique known as 'capnomancy', divination by smoke. As with the prophetic fire, it was principally the smoke from burnt offerings and sacrifices that was watched for omens. If the smoke was thin and wafted straight up, the portent was favourable. Apollonius of Tyana was said to have employed a form of capnomancy by throwing frankincense onto a sacrificial fire and noting not only the thickness of the smoke but how many 'points' it acquired, like the lucky or unlucky points of flame mentioned on the previous page. Also mentioned before was sideromancy, straws on hot iron, and there too the smoke was also read for an omen.

Because incense plays a vital role in so much eastern religious practice, the smoke of incense naturally found its way into capnomancy. In Malaya, in the past, a medicine man would use

Romans preparing to sacrifice a bull to their gods

smoke divination as part of a general rite to diagnose and cure illness. He would inhale the smoke, and if it smelt pleasant, the patient's recovery would be indicated. A scorched smell would cast doubt on his chances, and a foul smell would mean that he was beyond hope. Smoking often of course conferred the power of prophecy, supposedly, on shamans and priests and so on among other nations – like the hashish-smoking lands of North Africa, or the American Indians who used an extra strong and intoxicating tobacco – but these hallucinogenic effects are only distantly related to proper capnomancy.

Equally insubstantial with smoke are shadows, and primitive superstition tells us that a man's shadow contains an element of his soul. Some such belief may inform the old and uncommon practice of 'sciomancy', reading the future in omens from the darkness, definition and so on of shadows. Often the word is used to mean conjuring up spirits (shades) to prophesy, which is, as seen previously, better known as necromancy.

Making smoke for capnomancy

Mirror Magic

As the shadow was believed to contain one's soul (and sometimes other spirits), so mirrors can also be supernatural containers – hence the taboo against breaking them. Magic mirrors that impart useful information are notorious in folklore, from that of the queen in *Snow White* to those of the ancient Chinese who looked in them for signs of the demons that were causing specific illness or hardship. Catoptromancy, divination by mirrors, is a close relation of crystal gazing. Some say you always see spirits, and somehow cause them to foretell the future; otherwise you look for direct visions of the future as in the crystal or in the water surface of hydromancy. Water, indeed, can merge with mirrors: the Greeks used to lower a mirror into a sacred fountain at the temple of Ceres, to predict the outcome of an illness, and if a ghastly face appeared in the glass the patient was doomed. Or the mirror could combine with pyromancy: a church-blessed candle next to a mirror would (with special spells) cause the appearance in the glass of the face of a thief who was being sought.

Mirror gazing was often performed by staring at the reflection of moonlight in the glass. Comparably, Pythagoras recommended that mirrors should first be exposed to moonlight, to make them more efficient for divining. Not only glass mirrors were used: one might gaze into the shiny surfaces of swordblades, metal basins, a drop of clear oil on water, the back of watches, rings, anything silvered, and even someone else's eyeballs.

Mirrors were especially popular with mages at the close of the Middle Ages in Europe. Both Nostradamus and Agrippa are said to have used them, and the notorious Catherine de Medici apparently owned a magic mirror for divination. Such a mirror also appears in the Faust legend, as well as a host of less famous folktales of magic and devilry – and a good many old folk superstitions, providing rites by which a girl may see an image of her husband-to-be. Recently, though, as with hydromantic practices, the use of the mirror has been overtaken by the crystal ball, in common fortune telling.

Nostradamus showing the queen of France the images, in a magic mirror, of the nation's future rulers

Precious Stones

The use of jewels in divination, called lithomancy, recalls age-old superstitions about the magical properties of these special stones. Indeed, some were considered to have spirits of their own within them, fully aware and articulate, though the Roman writers and others who allude to this rarely elaborate on the magic required to make these spirits speak. Some medieval experts have mentioned that if certain jewels are dropped into water they emit a faint, high whistling that can be interpreted by the diviner.

Otherwise jewels instead of ordinary pebbles can be dropped into basins of water for the hydromantic technique that depends on counting ripples. The sapphire was especially favoured, though at other times the emerald and of course the diamond served admirably. Many ancient seers preferred to use their jewels as miniature crystal balls, to gaze into them for divinatory images. Many references are made to a supposed ancient Hebrew practice of divining by gazing into the twelve jewels on the breastplate (Ephod) of the 'high priest'. A tale put forward by Pliny mentioned a stone called 'anachitis' that can summon spirits to prophesy; another Roman writer asserted that a magic stone exists within the eyes of African hyenas which confers the prophetic gift on men.

Jewels have connections with astrology too, which gives them a back-door entrance into fortune telling; most people even today know their 'birthstone'. Then there is the parlour-game divination (if you have enough jewels) where you scatter the stones around a candle and note the first that reflects a wink of light at you. If it is a blue stone, good luck; green means a wish coming true, red means romance; violet means grief and yellow infidelity, grey means sadness and a garnet means a wedding.

'Margaritomancy' utilizes pearls — sometimes by reading the faint markings, but more often in a common old thief-finding rite. A pearl is placed in a closed container, with a spell or two uttered. Then names of suspects are spoken, and the pearl will leap and clatter (even, it is said, perforating the lid) at the true thief's name.

Fortune telling for the wealthy — omens from jewels

Mantic Miscellany

Hardly any aspect of man or nature has escaped use, as will have become obvious, in some form of divination; so a wholly comprehensive catalogue of the mantic arts would fill volumes. Within this more confined space, our limited catalogue can be wound up with mere allusions to a handful of the more rare, obscure, seldom used techniques. Take for example that which concerns itself with fingernails, called 'onychomancy', sometimes overlapping with the outer fringes of a palmist's job but more often being an offshoot of catoptromancy, for the fingernails are treated as mirrors and are gazed into for prophetic visions. The nail should be smoothed, perhaps waxed or oiled for extra shininess (sometimes with the chrism or holy oil); but other authorities from past centuries recommend blackening the nail with soot or ink, so as to see the vision as if through a glass darkly.

Usually the nails of an innocent child are used, just as such virgins were preferred to do the crystal or mirror gazing of past centuries. Children's nails might also be used for divination by means of spots or markings on the fingernails. This is also a useful do-it-yourself technique. White spots supposedly foretell happiness, if on the thumbnail; blue spots foreshadow misfortune, wherever they occur. The number of spots on the index finger enumerates your friends, those on the middle finger your enemies; spots on your ring fingernail mean a letter or a guest, on the little finger mean travel.

'Leconomancy' is the art of divining from shapes made by pouring oil upon water – less connected to hydromancy than to the reading of tea leaves, coffee grounds and the like. Just as obscure and extinct is the art of 'oenomancy', quite often used by the ancients, which interprets the shapes made by wine that is poured out in libations to the gods. 'Spodomancy' seeks fortunes revealed in the random patterns in ashes – sometimes from one's own fireplace, but more often from the ashes left from the burning of an offering to the gods (though this latter art is better known as 'tephromancy').

A fortune telling curiosity: in ancient Japan papers with written omens would be tied to a special tree, and the first to be blown off by the wind would reveal the future

Further Miscellany

The practice of 'amniomancy' must be one of the most unlikely, as well as uncommon, of the mantic arts. It is divination by the *caul,* that portion of the amniotic membrane from within the womb that sometimes remains attached to a newborn child. Cauls are of great value, for superstition says they protect the owner from drowning; they were bought and sold for this purpose within living memory. Diviners may read fortunes in the shapes of the thing; but more simply, at birth, if the caul is red the baby will have a fortunate life, but not so if the caul is grey.

At various times people have taken oracles from the outer shape or entrails of fish (ichthyomancy), from donkeys' heads (cephalomancy), from the movements of mice (myomancy) or snakes (ophiomancy), from the interiors of eggs revealed by candling (oomancy), from urine (uromancy) or faeces (scatomancy). They have read the future in laughter (geloscopy), and in the accidental meaningfulness of chance overheard remarks (cledonomancy). This last, as a way of obtaining an omen that is simpler even than bibliomancy, still seems a favourite among superstitious folk today.

Another remarkably unlikely technique from the past is 'alectryomancy', which has been given a measure of immortality because so many of the enemies of fortune telling like to display it as an example of ridiculous extremes. You draw a circle divided into sections for the letters of the alphabet. On each letter you place a grain, or grains, of corn. In the centre you place a cock, preferably loosely tied to keep it there (some say he should be black, others say white, still others believe it should be a hen). In any case, the omen emerges from the 'words' formed by the random order of letters at which the cock pecks. One is reminded of the response of a sceptical Roman emperor (some say Claudius) to the sacred chickens, whose eating habits similarly provided important omens. One day, when the emperor had certain plans, the birds ate nothing – a fatal sign. The emperor calmly picked them up and threw them into the river. If they would not eat, he said, why, let them drink.

A further curiosity: the process of alectryomancy

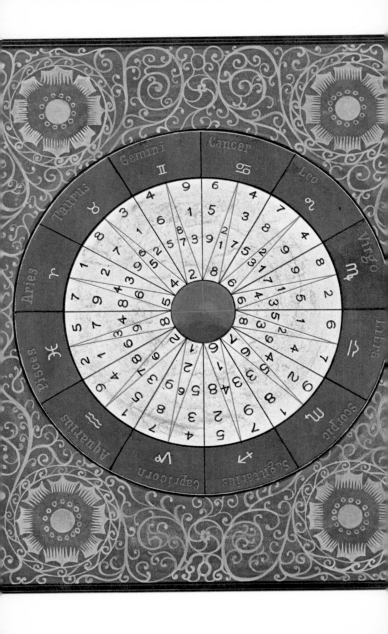

Modern Oddities

People today are so hungry to have their fortunes told, it would seem, that all the immense variety of history's mantic techniques is not enough. They have turned to technology, on one level or another, and married it to fortune telling – so that it is sometimes difficult to move in public without a divination dropping upon you. Match boxes and the like, in many countries, have fortunes printed upon them; weighing machines (especially in North America) spit out discreet tickets with a note of both your weight and your fortune; children find their futures spelled out on slips of paper in bubble gum packets, and so on. The fortunes told in these ways may all be of the vague, generalized kind like newspaper astrology: 'Success in romance may come your way but exercise caution in money matters', and that sort of thing. But people seem no less delighted to have them, and to perpetuate the means of their existence.

A great many of today's technological fortune-telling curiosities come in the form of instant astrology. There are machines (at British fun fairs, seaside resorts and so on) which offer to provide you with your horoscope if you turn a dial to your birth *month* and insert a coin. In Paris there was fairly recently a major department store providing a counter for off-the-cuff readings of customers' stars; in the United States there are more than 300 such stores with *computerized* horoscope services. American computers also produce rapid astrological readings on university campuses, by telephone in many cities, and from the 'Astroflash' booth in New York's Grand Central Station.

Then, as if all this was still not enough, individuals come up constantly with their own private forms of divination – from mere coin tossing to special personalized omens, like those alluded to in the opening pages of this book. So we come full circle, for out of such individual beliefs, at the dawn of history, came the fundamental omens that were systematized over millennia into all the major and minor forms of fortune telling.

A typical example of the fairly modern devices generically called 'Wheels of Fortune', to be spun and stopped for an omen. This one combines astrology and numerology

GREAT DIVINERS PAST AND PRESENT

Ancient Seers

Few of the priests or shamans who performed the ceremonial magic of the ancient religions have left their names in history. We remember instead the individuals, the odd men out who – as was generally accepted – had been gifted by the gods with their roles as seers and soothsayers.

It was not always an enjoyable gift. Remember that Cassandra of Troy was in legend blessed with the power of prophecy by Apollo, but with the non-blessed rider that no one would ever believe her. The Greek seer Tiresias, the myth says, was blinded and went through a sex change to earn his power – which he used to discover Oedipus as an incestuous parricide, and which he used even after his death when Odysseus summoned his ghost to prophesy.

The great Hebrew prophets of the Old Testament were hardly ordinary soothsayers: their inspiration made them defenders of the one true god and bearers of the Hebrew law –

Apollonius of Tyana, Cassandra and (right) Iamblichus

the conscience, as it were, of ancient Israel. Yet they foresaw the future, as Isaiah saw the coming decline of Judah, or as Jeremiah predicted the destruction of Jerusalem.

Many other names remain prominent in antiquity's roster of great seers — among them Artemidorus of Rome, compiler of a vast dream book mentioned before. None rose to such heights as Apollonius of Tyana, in the early years of the Christian era, soothsayer and worker of miracles around whom a cult sprang up that once threatened to rival Christianity itself. Apollonius is said to have foreseen the deaths of four Roman emperors including the assassination of Domitian, and also rightly predicted the rise to power of Vespasian. In the process he earned the enmity of the Roman priests and the early Christians, and eventually (the legend says) he was brought to trial on a trumped-up charge of human sacrifice, for his magical purposes. He foiled his accusers by miraculously vanishing from the court.

Medieval Mages

The so-called Dark Ages and Middle Ages of Europe were perhaps even more riddled with superstition than the declining days of the Roman Empire. Even on the highest level of intellectual attainment, a man who was a scholar would also inevitably be a student of the occult. Michael Scot, in the 13th century, wrote huge treatises on magic and divination, and served as astrologer to the Holy Roman Emperor Frederick II. He was not only student but practitioner, and is said to have predicted his own death, by a stone falling on his head. So he wore an iron skull-cap at all times – except when in church. And there one day a stone fell from the belfry and killed him.

Scot was also thought to be an expert conjurer of devils and necromancer, but he is best remembered for the influence of his writings on later mages. Among these was Albertus Magnus, said to be the most learned man of his time; and Roger Bacon, a notable experimenter who is claimed as a direct ancestor of modern science. Yet both men, like Scot, lent their enormous influence to the predominance of alchemy, astrology and divination generally in the syllabus of the medieval intellectual.

Then too (stretching the term 'medieval' somewhat) there was Cornelius Agrippa, sometime employee of the emperor Maximilian in the early 16th century, who proffered teachings in demonology and summoning spirits, and left great compilations of occult and divinatory lore. Paracelsus, also 16th century, was a physician whose alchemical work is hailed as vital to the early development of chemistry; but he was also devoted to astrology, herbalism and other magical matters, and wrote extensively on sortilege and clairvoyance. Unlike these, Dr John Dee, astrologer to Queen Elizabeth I, practised even more than he preached. He has been mentioned before as a legendary necromancer and operator of a famous crystal ball; his legend also credits him with having predicted the death of Mary Tudor, the execution of Mary Queen of Scots and the coming of the Spanish Armada.

Three major figures from the mediaeval and later heyday of occult scholarship: top to bottom, Agrippa (within a cabalistic seal), Paracelsus and Dr. John Dee

NOSTRADAMVS
1503-1566

Nostradamus

If Dee and the others are now just historical curiosities, re-calling something of the nature of their time, a French contemporary named Michel de Notre-Dame seems still to have direct relevance. Certainly the most celebrated diviner of the Christian era, Nostradamus was also a scholar and physician – and a fairly typical one, though his legend includes a few unlikely tales of miraculous cures. In 1555 he achieved world-wide fame when he published his predictions for the next few *centuries*, and the remainder of his own. They were expressed in verse quatrains of the most marvellously cryptic, allusive, oblique language imaginable, probably to protect himself from retaliation because of some dangerous predictions (regarding the death of kings and so on) about his own time. The verses make little clear sense until hindsight allows a comparison with events as they happened. But their difficulty has not baulked interpreters, in the 16th century or today when occult journals are clogged with 'explanations' of Nostradamus – mostly contradictory and often highly implausible.

The fame of Nostradamus took him, as astrologer and sage, to the court of Henry II and Catherine de Medici. The next ten years saw his eminence increase, though Henry died (and a quatrain seems to have foreseen that). Nostradamus himself died in 1566, and that too was apparently foreshadowed in a quatrain. Notwithstanding the difficulty of the verse, it is clear that many other apparent 'hits' have been made, and several of them seem to have been fairly closely dated. He predicted the fire of London in 1666, foresaw the French Revolution and specified many of its detailed occurrences including the flight of Louis XVI. He foresaw the English Civil War and Cromwell's advent, the rise and later career of Napoleon, and the activities of a later German leader, a 'destroyer', that admirably describes Hitler. Elsewhere, he says (or seems to say) that another destroyer or Antichrist will rise in 1999, to bring death and misery, a 'yellow invasion' of Europe, and the end of civilization as we know it. Armageddon, however, is not due until after the year 7000.

Nostradamus, physician, magician and diviner, whose cryptic prophecies still create controversy and attract believers

Later Marvels

The 18th century liked to think of itself as an 'Age of Reason', devoted to science and common sense, free from the superstition of previous times. Out of all that rationality came the curious figure of Count Cagliostro, a flamboyant Italian who was either adulated as a mage or denounced as a fraud. He was famed as a healer and alchemist (using the latter art, we are told, to create a vast diamond for a cardinal); yet at various times he was expelled from Russia and imprisoned in the Bastille in Paris. As a diviner, he seems to have relied on clairvoyance, but dressed it up in 'séances' where a young virgin girl gazed on his behalf into crystal balls or bottles of water. In England, he convinced many of his powers by consistently winning lotteries; in Europe, it was said that he accurately predicted the death of the empress Maria Theresa in 1780.

The next century was also fairly smug about its hardheaded scientific rationalism, but managed to give birth to theosophy, spiritualism and other occult systems, as well as a vast renaissance for divination. Among its leading occultists was a French magician named Constant who called himself Eliphas Lévi. Noted especially for his compilations of ceremonial magic, Lévi was also a notable operator of the Tarot cards and is remembered for a legendary conjuration of a spirit – either Apollonius or Agrippa, depending on which account you read, though they all mention that Lévi fainted with terror before he could ask the apparition to prophesy.

Later in the 19th century the western world saw a remarkable upsurge in the prominence of astrology, palmistry and the other forms of divination that still rank high. Men like 'Zadkiel' (R. J. Morrison) in England rose to fame along with these practices. Zadkiel's almanac, rich in astrology, remained a best-seller for years and was perpetuated – with the pseudonym – long after his death. Count Louis Hamon as 'Cheiro' did the same popularizing job for palmistry, largely by his accurate predictions of such events as Queen Victoria's death, Lord Kitchener's death, and more.

Assorted famous fortune telling names from more recent centuries: top to bottom, Evangeline Adams, Count Cagliostro and Eliphas Lévi with a mystical diagram

EVANGELINE ADAMS

Modern Prognosticators

When both fortune telling and public relations have become big business, and have got together, as in recent years, it becomes nearly impossible to single out individual diviners as the best known. But many authorities would probably include, near the top of the list if not at it, the late Edgar Cayce, American healer and clairvoyant. Known as the 'sleeping prophet' because he operated from a trance state, Cayce as healer frequently diagnosed illnesses and prescribed medicaments in terms that he would not have consciously understood. Some of his cures were mostly miraculous, including his saving of his son's eyesight when doctors had given up hope. Equally successful as a seer, Cayce is said to have predicted the 1929 stock market crash, the onset of World War II, a 1964 earthquake in Alaska, and much more. He died in 1945 (having predicted the date), but not without warning of the imminence of worldwide natural and geological catastrophe that would last for 40 years.

Left to right, Edgar Cayce, Maurice Woodruff, Jean Dixon

Notable among living seers is the British astrologer and clairvoyant Maurice Woodruff, son of a famous clairvoyant mother who once predicted the present Duke of Windsor's marriage. Woodruff himself has been credited with foreseeing both the Kennedy and Johnson presidencies and the accession of Cassius Clay as he then was to the heavyweight crown. In 1970 he ventured to predict Ronald Reagan's imminent loss of the California governorship, and Nixon's landslide re-election in 1972.

Also given to political prognostication is the Washington seer Jean Dixon whose immense fame is based on her prediction of John Kennedy's assassination: she correctly foresaw that a blue-eyed Democrat elected president in 1960 would be killed in office. She is said also to have predicted the time of death of Roosevelt, and to have risked much by predicting Churchill's loss of the 1945 British elections, a possibility then undreamed of. Recently she has foreseen a major war against China for 1980, and an era of world peace opening after 1999 (contradicting Nostradamus).

DIVINATION AND SCIENCE

There are other modern prognosticators whose arts are not occult, and who would not consider themselves to be seers. They are the people who use accepted scientific procedures to predict future events to a high degree of probability. We know especially those who impinge directly on our lives. Take the so-called weathermen, not just the broadcasters but the meteorologists behind them. Meteorology is a highly developed science, especially now that satellite photography can show half the world's weather at once, and all the likely movements of warm or cold fronts, low and high pressure areas and the rest. All this should make prediction, especially short-term, fairly safe. Yet the weather remains unpredictable: in 1971 Britain was promised, on the best authority, a heat-wave in June, and so people were understandably disappointed and annoyed by the time the third week of steady June rainfall had got under way.

Computers and high-powered statistical techniques have given a boost recently to the art of predicting elections, or doing market research, or other processes requiring the sampling of public opinion. So the debacle of 1948, when Harry Truman became President in the face of all the opinion polls, should never have happened again. But in 1969 the computers predicted a comfortable victory for the British Labour party, which turned overnight into a Conservative win that left the psephologists speechless.

In the same way sudden flights of money, due to speculation, from one nation to another, or sudden stock-market fluctuations, give the lie to the confident predictions of economists and their computers. Perhaps only in medicine has science become sure in its foresight. Doctors can not only predict accurately the sex of an unborn child, but can tell much else – some of it mildly frightening, such as (from an examination of the chromosomes) whether it has criminal proclivities. Or so, anyway, statistics seem to show.

Meteorology is today an exact science, with weather photography from satellites and computerisation – yet its predictions day by day can still go badly awry

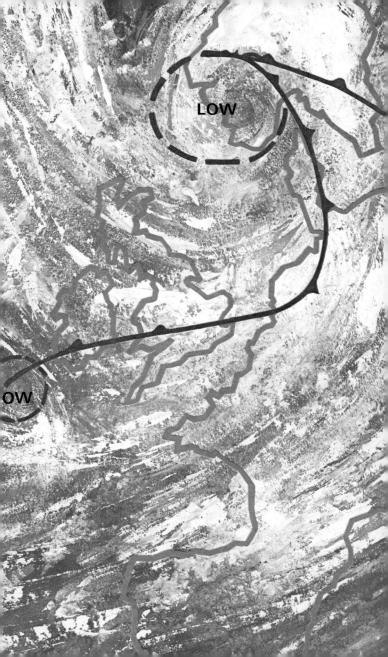

Chance and Probability

Common sense tells us that there are two forces operating on patterns of events in this world – chance and causality. If I strike a match and it lights, that is causality, cause and effect. If I strike a match and somewhere in Tasmania at that moment a house catches fire, that is chance, coincidence. Occultists see causality in things like magic working or accurate prediction of the future by stars or palms or cards; rationalists see coincidence. C. G. Jung, as said before, looked for a middle ground in his idea of 'meaningful coincidence', synchronicity, but the obscurities of this theory make it as yet inaccessible to the layman.

Statisticians can measure chance: mathematics can express the probability of an event, or a sequence of events. But while in the laboratory these probabilities can be unimaginably accurate, out in the world statistics are no surer than plain guesses. Gamblers know that the chances of, say, drawing a fourth ace to a hand of three are minute, but it has happened. Wild chances do come off, weird coincidences are always

happening (the more so if you are watching for them). Must there be any meaningful conclusions to be drawn? Can we look to occurrences that smack very much of random accident for a firm foundation to a belief in magic and divination? All things may be possible in the long run, even a chimpanzee typing out Shakespeare's plays, but in those terms the long run has become nearly infinite, and irrelevant to human life. So we are left with the two camps nowhere near reconciliation. The one crying 'coincidence' when a prediction comes true – or asserting that the prediction was so vaguely phrased that only hindsight made it true – or asserting that the subject's suggestibility made the prophecy about him come true – or whatever. The other camp trotting out its case histories, accounts of predictions that did come true (often astoundingly authenticated), its scientific or quasi-scientific rationalizations of method, or whatever. Perhaps one day some genius will invent a technique that will find proof or disproof. Until then, as regards fortune telling, today as in the Stone Age, you pays your money and you takes your choice.

Computers can estimate probability to incredible accuracy

BOOKS TO READ

History of Magic by Kurt Seligmann. Pantheon Books, New York, 1948.

The Black Arts by Richard Cavendish. Routledge and Kegan Paul, London, 1968.

Magic and Superstition by Douglas Hill. Paul Hamlyn, London, 1968.

Prophets and Prediction by Richard Lewinsohn. Secker and Warburg, London, 1961.

The Story of Fulfilled Prophecy by Justine Glass. Cassell, London, 1969.

Book of Fortune-Telling by Sybil Leek. W. H. Allen, London, 1970.

Astrology by Louis MacNeice. Aldus Books, London, 1964.

The Book of the Hand by Fred Gettings. Paul Hamlyn, London, 1965.

INDEX

TITLES IN THIS SERIES

Arts
Art Nouveau for Collectors/Collecting and Looking After Antiques/Collecting Inexpensive Antiques/Silver for Collectors/ Toys and Dolls for Collectors

Domestic Animals and Pets
Cats/Dog Care/Dogs/Horses and Ponies/Tropical Freshwater Aquaria/Tropical Marine Aquaria

Gardening
Flower Arranging/Garden Flowers/Garden Shrubs/House Plants

General Information
Aircraft/Beachcombing and Beachcraft/Espionage/Freshwater Fishing/Modern Combat Aircraft/Modern First Aid/Photography/ Sailing/Sea Fishing/Trains/Wargames

History and Mythology
Witchcraft and Black Magic

Natural History
Bird Behaviour/Birds of Prey/Birdwatching/Butterflies/Fishes of the World/Fossils and Fossil Collecting/A Guide to the Seashore/ Prehistoric Animals/Seabirds/Seashells/Trees of the World

Popular Science
Astrology/Astronomy/Biology/Computers at Work/Ecology/ Economics/Electricity/Electronics/Exploring the Planets/Geology/ The Human Body/Microscopes and Microscopic Life/Psychology/ Rocks, Minerals and Crystals/The Weather Guide